ENOUGH CHAOS

Volume Two

GLEN PENN

CLAY BRIDGES
P R E S S

Enough Chaos
Volume Two

Copyright © 2022 by Glen Penn

Published by Clay Bridges in Houston, TX
www.claybridgespress.com

Unless otherwise indicated, all Scripture quotations are taken from the New American Standard Bible® (NASB), Copyright © 1960, 1962, 1963, 1968, 1971, 1972, 1973, 1975, 1977, 1995 by The Lockman Foundation. Used by permission. www.Lockman.org.

Scripture quotations marked (ESV) are taken from the ESV® Bible (The Holy Bible, English Standard Version®), copyright © 2001 by Crossway, a publishing ministry of Good News Publishers. Used by permission. All rights reserved.

Scripture quotations marked (NKJV) are taken from the New King James Version®. Copyright © 1982 by Thomas Nelson. Used by permission. All rights reserved.

Scripture quotations marked (KJV) are taken from the King James Version (KJV): King James Version, public domain.

Scripture quotations marked (NIV) are taken from the Holy Bible, New International Version®, NIV®. Copyright ©1973, 1978, 1984, 2011 by Biblica, Inc.™ Used by permission of Zondervan. All rights reserved worldwide. www.zondervan.com The "NIV" and "New International Version" are trademarks registered in the United States Patent and Trademark Office by Biblica, Inc.™

eISBN: 978-1-68488-033-1
ISBN: 978-1-68488-032-4

Special Sales: Most Clay Bridges titles are available in special quantity discounts. Custom imprinting or excerpting can also be done to fit special needs. For standard bulk orders, go to www.claybridgesbulk.com. For specialty press or large orders, contact Clay Bridges at info@claybridgespress.com.

DEDICATION

I dedicate this book to God. All glory to the highest power. I am not perfect. God is. If you read this and something unlocks in your mind, God did that, not me. If you grow in your understanding, God did this, not me. If you become a better servant because of something you read here, God did this, not me. *All* glory to God.

I also dedicate this book to every "giant" I have stood upon. God, Christ, and Spirit are my King, but these boys and girls sure do stand tall—a hippie in Afghanistan, a peaceful man in Richmond, Texas, a loving childcare director at church, and a woman who saw past the punk kid I was. These are just a few of them. To all the unsung heroes of my past, I lovingly thank you for believing in me, teaching me, and sometimes . . . fussin' at me.

TABLE OF CONTENTS

PREFACE

I want to start by stating some ideals on which this book was written.

1. Both spiritually and logically, I am on a search for truth. I want to know the truest statement. That sounds weird, but I believe the truth has varying degrees of truth. A lie is a lie, but the truth is a scale. The scale starts with God's truth, which is absolute, and then there is our truth, which is not always complete. The trick in finding the truth is to have more information. Jimmy is a boy. That is true. Jimmy is a Southern boy who is eight years old, loves baseball and apple pie, and hates it when his dog is sick because Spike is his best friend. The first statement is true—Jimmy is a boy. But I believe the second statement is truer because it has more truths in it. It paints a better picture. For much of my life, I needed only the simple truth. The electric bill is due on the 30th of every month. Simple truth. But for my relationships, including my relationship with God, I crave the truest statements. I want to know everything I can in order to do better, love

better, and serve better. This book is intended to help anyone on the road I was on.

2. We are all standing on the shoulders of giants. Some say Bernard of Chartres said that and others say it was Isaac Newton, but that doesn't matter to me. I believe the statement is true. A truer statement is that we are all standing on the written thoughts and works of all who came before us. And if I screwed something up in this book or misquoted someone, please do not fail to see the beauty because your glasses are too dark. I don't expect anyone to agree with everything in this book, but I do believe everything in this book is true. If you have a truer version, I would embrace that thought. If you believe the words are a lie, that is your choice. But I believe in the truth.

3. I believe the King James Version of the Bible is the truest version of the Bible, and I believe the Bible is true. The New American Standard Bible is my second favorite version of the Bible. I always try to refer to Blue Letter Bible online and *Strong's Concordance*. I like that Blue Letter Bible puts all the translations next to each other. God gave me the right to choose (eat the fruit, don't eat the fruit), and I love, love, love anyone and anything that gives me the right to choose what I think is right for me, following the example of *my God*. Give me the facts, and leave me be. My spirit will measure the truth and get back to you. Obviously, I would never speak to my King this way, because he gave me the options before I could have had that thought. He

gave me the right to choose, and I love people who follow his example. Due to copyright restrictions, have used several versions of the Bible in this book, including the New American Standard Version (NASB 1995), the English Standard Version (ESV), the New King James Version (NKJV), and the King James Version (KJV).

4. I love people and hate sin. I have seen the darkness. If you haven't seen the darkness, this statement probably doesn't make much sense, but for those who have seen the darkness, I can tell you it is in the eyes of mankind, it is in the smell of burning flesh, it is in evil deeds. The darkness is not a person, but I believe everyone has the ability to touch the darkness. Some are consumed by the darkness. Some will always be consumed by it. Only God knows what is in a man's or a woman's future. I do not blame a sinner for sinning. I believe we are to be helping each other clean the muck off our feet, but we are all fat with destructive self-interest—and we can't reach our own feet. We need other good (godly) men and women to help us recognize when our feet are dirty. I will dive into this rambling later on in a chapter, but I do not blame the darkness for being dark. I accept sin for sin, and I try to wash people's feet. Many will I attempt to help, but few will let me.

5. The start of this wasn't a book at all. It was just a notebook that helped me keep all my thoughts together. Other books like the legendary *Strong's Concordance* are phenomenal in their tedious

attention, but holy rusted metal batman, they are massive. Their biggest downfall for me is that I have to keep flipping around in my Bible to find the passages they are talking about. This is not a flaw in their design. They are perfect for what they are intended to do. I wanted something I could use to answer questions with minimal breaks in the action. I wanted less search time. So I started with a topic and hand-wrote everything I could find in the Bible that was relevant to that specific topic. I wanted someone to be able to ask me a question and I did not have to pull out my Bible unless the Spirit told me to. Is it good to memorize the entire Bible? Yes! But my memory of where those verses are sucks. I can't remember birthdays, either. I can remember the idea of the scripture, but where did I read it? In the Bible . . . um . . . ah . . . near the middle, I think. That is why I made my notebook. I showed it to a friend one day during a Bible study, and he got all excited and asked for a copy. That notebook evolved into this—all Spirit-led.

6. Most important, I am not a great man. I am a sinner. I have sinned more than most. I have done terrible things. I have been given grace, and now I strive to live by my Father's words. I fail. I sin every day. Sometimes I reach for the Oreos when I should reach for my barbells. Sometimes I see a pretty lady and have a bad thought. Sometimes I see an ugly lady and have a bad thought. Sometimes my son acts like a 12-year-old boy, which he is right at this moment, and I am harsher than I should be with

him. The mark of my faith is that once my sin is past, I fall back on my knees, ask for forgiveness, and try to make amends to those I have sinned against. I am not perfect, and I still have blemishes, but the Spirit, Jesus, God, and I are working on that. The measure of a man is not how hard he can punch but how hard he can get hit and keep moving forward. My prayer for this world and each of you is that no matter how hard you get hit (even from yourself) you will keep moving forward to God. Some steps are tiny. Some steps are leaps. Stay alert, stay alive, and keep moving forward.

7. Some of this book is my own findings. Some are my findings with my commentary. Some are just my ramblings on how I understand a specific topic. I do not expect anyone to completely agree with everything I say. I can take 100 people and have them paint a picture of a flower, and guess what? None of the flowers will be exactly the same. I am painting a picture of my understanding. If you don't like it, that is your choice, and I still love you.

8. If you have a problem with something I have written, I suggest you consider the source of your problem. If you have a problem with the words written in the Bible, that is between you and the Bible (God, in my opinion). If you have a problem with my understanding, I will love it because it allows me to grow, and maybe, just maybe, you can get my feet cleaner. I know that sounds selfish, but I am selfish. We are all selfish. We start life crying out for food, and in my opinion, we still are. We just

learned to cry out more quietly. If your problem is with the Bible and you want to fight just to fight, I am not interested. If you want to troll and criticize because people believe in things and you believe in nothing, I am not interested. I loved the debate between Bill Nye and Ken Ham. I love science, and I love to understand how things were made and how they interact. I love the idea of receiving new information that alters my understanding. I love putting together the puzzle of what God wants for me. I do not love "chewers." I define chewers as people who chew up other people just to exercise their teeth. They are big men and women who intentionally stay in small pools because they like the power of chewing up the smaller fish. They are people who go on social media and comment solely to spread hate, chew up people, or piss people off so other people will look at them like *big fish*. The chewer worm-tongues in the world that will never take the mantle of true leadership and lead their people to godly health and godly love but will always point out the failures of their leaders and weaknesses of their peers to spread the seeds of corruption with every breath they take. If you have a problem with your leadership, rise up and lead. I hate chewers, and I will not indulge you— ever. The wolf is the wolf, and I can respect it even if I have to kill it to keep my flock safe. The sheep are the sheep, and I can respect them for they love to eat grass and make babies. The chewers, in my opinion, are the insects that stay hidden until the real predators and prey are gone, and then they dine on the corrupted meat and animal droppings and the hard work of the previous inhabitants of the area. If you want to have a debate in the interest of my convincing you or your convincing me, great. If you are earnestly on a truth mission, so am I, and let's compare notes. If I have said something confusing to you, please allow me the opportunity to explain it better or more extensively. If all you want to do is bring things down and topple people and avenge the wrongdoings that people have committed against you, I am not interested. Revenge is never satisfying, and people shouldn't act like a virus. I am not interested in talking to you. I have my mission and my gifts. Dealing with chewers is undoubtedly someone else's mission, but I will pray for you. My Christ is stronger, better, and smarter than I am, and you should try talking to him. Mr. or Mrs. Big Fish.

With all the love possible, eat up, boys and girls, 'cause Daddy has made us a feast.

—Glen Penn

TABLE OF CONTENTS

(This Table of Contents for Volume 1 is included to provide a quick reference when hunting for a section throughout the *Enough Chaos* works.)

NEPHILIM: ANGELS HAVING SEX THEORY

Why is this important?

If the view I am countering is true, then God slaughters the innocent . . . a lot of them. Gimme some rope, and I will show you.

There is a *large* group of people who believe something. I will give you the main verses they use to support that view.

> *Now it came about when men began to multiply on the face of the land, and daughters were born to them, that the sons of God saw that the daughters of men were beautiful; and they took wives for themselves, whomever they chose. Then the Lord said, "My Spirit shall not strive with man forever, because he also is flesh; nevertheless his days shall be one hundred and twenty years." The Nephilim were on the earth in those days, and also afterward when the sons of God came into the daughters of men, and they bore children to them. Those were the mighty men who were of old, men of renown.*

1

Then the Lord saw that the wickedness of man was great on the earth and that every intent of the thoughts of his heart was only evil continually. The Lord was sorry that He had made man on the earth, and He was grieved in His heart. The Lord said, "I will blot out man whom I have created from the face of the land, from man to animals to creeping things and to birds of the sky; for I am sorry that I have made them." But Noah found favor in the eyes of the Lord.

Now the earth was corrupt in the sight of God, and the earth was filled with violence. God looked on the earth, and behold, it was corrupt; for all flesh had corrupted their way upon the earth.

Then God said to Noah, "The end of all flesh has come before Me; for the earth is filled with violence because of them; and behold, I am about to destroy them with the earth. Make for yourself an ark of gopher wood; you shall make the ark with rooms, and shall cover it inside and out with pitch.

—Gen. 6:1–8, 11–14

These are the main verses people use to prop up the idea that angels fell from heaven, had sex with human women, and created the Nephilim "race." There are other supporting verses that I will address later, but this is the main event.

If you *do not* believe this is true, good. Me too. But you may come into contact with an angels-have-sex believer.

If you do believe in this theory, please grab a Coke, get comfy, and let's break this down.

First, God Would Be an Innocent Slayer

If angels hooked up with human women . . . and God got pissed and flooded the world because of it . . . let me ask you this: What did human men do to deserve this wrath? A global flood is something I would say qualifies as God's wrath. What did these males do?

You see, when God punishes, he punishes people very specifically.

Take the Garden of Eden story. The snake did his part, Adam did his part, and Eve did her part. So did God punish them unequally?

> *The Lord God said to the serpent,*
> *"Because you have done this,*
> *Cursed are you more than all cattle,*
> *And more than every beast of the field;*
> *On your belly you will go,*
> *And dust you will eat*
> *All the days of your life;*
> *And I will put enmity*
> *Between you and the woman,*
> *And between your seed and her seed;*
> *He shall bruise you on the head,*
> *And you shall bruise him on the heel."*
>
> —Gen. 3:14–15

The snake tempted Eve, and he got punished, right? The enmity spoken of here is that the future coming of Christ will lead the good away while the followers of sin will remain. There will be more on this in another book.

3

To the woman He said,
"I will greatly multiply
Your pain in childbirth,
In pain you will bring forth children;
Yet your desire will be for your husband,
And he will rule over you."

—Gen. 3:16

Eve ate the fruit and gave some to Adam. Did she get punished? Yes.

Then to Adam, He said, "Because you have listened to the voice of your wife, and have eaten from the tree about which I commanded you, saying, 'You shall not eat from it';
Cursed is the ground because of you;
In toil you will eat of it
All the days of your life.
Both thorns and thistles it shall grow for you;
And you will eat the plants of the field;
By the sweat of your face
You will eat bread,
Till you return to the ground,
Because from it you were taken;
For you are dust,
And to dust you shall return."

—Gen. 3:17–19

Man ate the fruit, blame-shifted to Eve, and then stood defiant toward God. Did he get punished? Yes.

Now take this same principle, and three chapters—not books—later, we have this.

> *The Lord said, "I will blot out man whom I have created from the face of the land, from man to animals to creeping things and to birds of the sky; for I am sorry that I have made them."*

—Gen. 6:7

Do you see *angel*? Do you even see *woman*? Nope.

According to BlueLetterBible.com (*Strong's Concordance* reference number H120), this is translated as Adam, which means either the actual human male named Adam, men in general, or all of humankind. *Nowhere* is it suggested that it means female humans only or angels. The word is *man*.

So again, I ask you, what did men do wrong?

My God punishes justly. I'm not sure what your God does?

The Second Issue Is Pattern

What makes more sense?

Genesis 4:1–15:	Cain and Abel (Abel is killed)
Genesis 4:16–24	Cain's bloodline
Genesis 4:25–26	Seth is born
Genesis 5	Seth's bloodline
Genesis 6	Seth and Cain's bloodlines mix

or

Genesis 4:1–15:	Cain and Abel (Abel is killed)
Genesis 4:16–24	Cain's bloodline
Genesis 4:25–26	Seth is born

Genesis 5   Seth's bloodline
Genesis 6   Angels have sex with humans

See? The pattern doesn't fit.

Maybe all the "fluff" is distracting, so I will show it to you broken down in simple terms.

Cain and Abel
Cain's bloodline
Seth is born
Seth's bloodline
Seth and Cain's bloodlines mix

or

Cain and Abel
Cain's bloodline
Seth is born
Seth's bloodline
Angels have sex with humans

Can you see it? When you pull all the crazy smoke and mirrors away from preachers' productions and serpentine twisting of Scripture, things become abundantly clear.

My God repeats himself and foreshadows and has hindsight. I'm not sure what your God does.

Third, Look at the Words! Look! Look!

The Nephilim were on the earth in those days, and also afterward when the sons of God came into the daughters *of men, and they bore children to them. Those were the mighty men who were **of old, men of renown.***

—Gen. 6:4

They were *already* on earth and *also after.*
Those were the "mighty men."
Let's have a look at who the Bible says are mighty men.

Gen. 6:4	Exod. 15:15	Josh. 6:2	Josh. 8:3
Josh. 10:2	Josh. 10:7	Judg. 6:12	Judg. 11:1
Ruth 2:1	1 Sam. 2:4	1 Sam. 9:1	1 Sam. 16:18
2 Sam. 16:16	2 Sam. 17:8	2 Sam. 17:10	2 Sam. 20:7
2 Sam. 23:8	2 Sam. 23:9	2 Sam 23:16	2 Sam. 23:17
2 Sam. 23:22	1 Kings 1:8	1 Kings 1:10	1 Kings 11:28
2 Kings 5:1	2 Kings 15:20	2 Kings 24:14	1 Chron. 1:15
1 Chron. 5:24	1 Chron. 7:7	1 Chron. 7:9	1 Chron. 7:11
1 Chron. 7:40	1 Chron. 8:40	1 Chron. 11:10	1 Chron. 11:11
1 Chron. 12:1	1 Chron. 12:4	1 Chron. 12:21	1 Chron. 12:25
1 Chron. 12:30	1 Chron. 19:8	1 Chron. 26:6	1 Chron. 26:31
1 Chron. 28:1	1 Chron. 29:24	2 Chron. 13:3	2 Chron. 14:8
2 Chron. 17:13	2 Chron. 17:14	2 Chron. 17:16	2 Chron. 17:17
2 Chron. 25:6	2 Chron. 26:12	2 Chron. 28:7	2 Chron. 32:3
Neh. 11:14	Job 22:8	Jer. 48:14	Lam. 1:15
Ezek. 32:12	Ezek. 39:18	Ezek. 39:20	Rev. 6:15
Rev. 19:18			

Whooee! That was an exhaustive list.

You see, partners, if God brought a flood to kill the Nephilim who became the "mighty men of old," he is not very good at killing. My God is an expert at life and death, things he created. I don't know who your God is.

Nephilim just means *men of renown*. There is a place in the Bible where these specific men of renown were described as really, really tall. This is merely a term meaning a "special person." Boaz, the husband of Ruth, was called a "mighty man of wealth." It just means men of renown, special people. David had his "mighty men." Why didn't God wipe them out? It just means super-special people.

The other thing we pull from the readings is this: How many people stepped off the ark?

There were eight people according to Scripture.

Then Noah and his sons and his wife and his sons' wives with him entered the ark because of the water of the flood.

—Gen. 7:7

Noah and his wife.
Ham and his wife.
Shem and his wife.
Japeth and his wife.

Through mitochondrial DNA and Y chromosomes, we can track our genetics back to a bottleneck of a common *male* more recent than a common *female,* and science is stumped. They keep rerunning the dates. Poor people. Bless their hearts.

Science, your data is not wrong. Your understanding of the years and life spans is, but not the data. You are not factoring in the longer life and purer DNA. I know the names of those ancestors that bottleneck you—Noah a long time ago and Eve an even longer time ago.

Noah's sons all had his Y chromosomes, but his sons' wives had the genetics of their parents. Thus, Eve would be the most logical bottleneck point above that (or a female directly below her). Told ya'll, I love science.

The reason I bring this up is that either the Nephilim survived outside the ark during the flood (which we have *zero* biblical evidence for and would make the flood *completely pointless*), or we are talking about normal human DNA genetic mutations like being tall, like being really tall.

The tallest person in modern history was Robert Wadlow, 1940, who stood 8 feet 11 inches.

But we also need to bring in cellular degradation. What does that mean, Professor Glen? I am glad you asked.

Think of it as taking a crystal-clear print of your favorite band's flyer and making a copy of it. It comes out a little less clear, right? Then make a copy of that copy. And do it again and again.

The non-Christian 1996 movie *Multiplicity* starring Michael Keaton and Andie MacDowell explored this concept regarding human cloning.

Females (other than Sara in the Bible) have a limited window to have children, but males keep "taking part" well into their old age. It is rumored that a 94-year-old man fathered a kid, but that is the Internet for you. Do your research. You will see that it happens well past a man's 80s. Why is that important? It is because of cellular degradation.

When I gave you the copy-of-a-copy example, I wasn't referring to a father-to-son passing of DNA. I was referring to the bazillions of times a man's cells copy and divide within his own body. That results in things such as cancer, poor eyesight, grey hair, saggy *things*, hair where it shouldn't be— essentially "getting old." That is because the cells have divided many times, and each time, they change just a smidgeon. Multiply a smidgeon changes by the age of the father, and you will get some *very* altered DNA compared to his DNA in his 20s.

Father	Age at Conception	Son
Adam	130	Seth
Seth	105	Enos
Enos	90	Cainam
Cainam	70	Mahalaleel
Mahalaleel	65	Jared
Jared	162	Enoch
Enoch	65	Methuselah
Methuselah	187	Lamech
Lamech	182	Noah

I stop at Noah because we are not certain if Ham, Shem, or Japheth carried the Nephilim DNA trait. But it is likely that Noah and at least one of his sons did. True, it could have come solely from one of the females on the big boat, but it is guaranteed to have passed to at least one of Noah's grandchildren. There is a minor chance that the human DNA pool just mutated again and Moses (author of Genesis) is recognizing that here. Either way, Nephilim were here before the flood *and* after.

So we need to remember that Adam's body was created perfectly, and he ate the good fruit of the Garden of Eden. That means he was an amazing specimen of our genetics. Theoretically, as death wasn't a thing yet, he was immortal, either because of his body *or* because of the good fruit of the garden. But the point of origin is pointless because the fall of man did happen, and our genetic DNA degradation started.

How do we know that? Because Adam died when he was 930 years old. Modern science says that is impossible, but I can clearly see—and most geneticists will agree either in part or totally—that we are genetically decomposing as a species. Our eyesight is getting poorer. Cancer cases are on the rise. Migraine headaches, back pains, sexually transmitted diseases, even the flu—everything—is getting worse, not better. Darwin and modern science say things should be getting better, but that is not what we are seeing, not as Christians, not as scientists, not as ecologists. Nothing is getting better.

Wow! What a long rabbit hole! Reread this if you need to. That was a lot of scientific mumbo-jumbo, and I do apologize to both the readers and the science nerds who are ripping me up for my terminology (Is the overview correct? Okay then).

Why is this important?

Because . . .

Then a champion came out from the armies of the Philistines, named Goliath, from Gath, whose height was six cubits and a span.

—1 Sam. 17:4

Goliath. Yes, that Goliath was 9 feet 9 inches tall. If we had purer DNA and more years for degradation, that kind of height might easily be possible today.

*So they gave out to the sons of Israel a bad report of the land which they had spied out, saying, "The land through which we have gone, in spying it out, is a land that devours its inhabitants; and all the people whom we saw in it are men of great **size.** There also we saw the Nephilim (the sons of Anak are part of the Nephilim);*

11

and we became like grasshoppers in our own sight, and so we were in their sight."

—Num. 13:32–33

These were tall, tall men . . . who were here *after the flood.*

If you dispute this, then riddle me this, Batman: which person who came off the ark was an angel-human hybrid? It doesn't make sense. This theory is false, my family. False.

When my God wants you dead, you die. I'm not sure what your God does.

What Does the New Testament Say?

For to which of the angels did He ever say,
"You are My Son,
Today I have begotten You"?
And again,
"I will be a Father to Him
And He shall be a Son to Me"?

—Heb. 1:5

Ugh! Oh! Looks like God has made it *very* clear that the angels are *not* his sons. But keep in mind that he is referring to Christ/Son, not other sons. Capitol "S" is used in this meaning.

But are Christians his sons?

But those who are considered worthy to attain to that age and the resurrection from the dead, neither marry nor are given in marriage; for they cannot even die anymore, because they are like angels, and are sons of God, being sons of the resurrection.

—Luke 20:35–36

Angels cannot die. True Christians cannot die *and* are sons of God. If angels were considered sons of God, it wouldn't have been worded this way. Angels are not the sons of the resurrection. They are not. That word is referring to true Christians, not angels. They are like this *and* have this other trait too.

For all who are being led by the Spirit of God, these are sons of God.

—Rom. 8:14

We, true Christians, are sons of God.

But Glen! Christians weren't around back in the days of Genesis. True, my brothers and mothers (bros and mos). But there was a group of people he considered his children, even back then.

For thus says the Lord,
"Sing aloud with gladness for Jacob,
And shout among the chief of the nations;
Proclaim, give praise and say,
'O Lord, save Your people,
The remnant of Israel '
Behold, I am bringing them from the north country,
And I will gather them from the remote parts of the earth,
Among them the blind and the lame,
The woman with child and she who is in labor with child,
together;
A great company, they will return here.
With weeping they will come,
And by supplication I will lead them;
I will make them walk by streams of waters,

On a straight path in which they will not stumble;
For I am a father to Israel,
And Ephraim is My firstborn."

—Jer. 31:7–9

Okay, so Israel is the children of God, and their males are sons of God.

For in Him we live and move and exist, as even some poets have said, "For we also are His children." Being then the children of God, we ought not to think that the Divine Nature is like gold or silver or stone, an image formed by the art and thought of man.

—Acts 17:28–29

According to Scripture, there are three main groups of people: Christians, Israelites, and any human who "lives and moves and exists" in God. Keep in mind, this is not a current set of paths determined by life choices, but rather a divine timing set of paths. BEFORE the coming of Christ, the path was Israel. Before the formation of Israel, the path was simple obedience (Adam, Eve, and Noah for example). But all three groups, in their own timing with God, had to live, move, and exist in God.

What did God think of Noah?

But Noah found favor in the eyes of the Lord.

—Gen. 6:8

But couldn't this be just God pitying Noah? No. Noah was a God-loving man, according to the Big Book.

And did not spare the ancient world, but preserved Noah, a preacher of righteousness, with seven others, when He brought a flood upon the world of the ungodly.

—2 Pet. 2:5

By faith Noah, being warned by God about things not yet seen, in reverence prepared an ark for the salvation of his household, by which he condemned the world, and became an heir of the righteousness which is according to faith

—Heb. 11:7

Conclusion

The sons of God, spoken of during the times of Noah, were all the men who were following God and then turned away, lured by women of other tribes who were not following God. They walked away from following God and got extremely violent. God didn't punish *men* because of angels. He punished men and women because of men and women. Was it really because of their violence?

Now the earth was corrupt in the sight of God, and the earth was filled with violence.

—Gen. 6:11

And did not spare the ancient world, but preserved Noah, a preacher of righteousness, with seven others, when He brought a flood upon the world of the ungodly.

—2 Pet. 2:5

They were killing each other—wholesale. I imagine murder was probably one of the lesser crimes in those days. There are things much more diabolical and evil than murder. Sometimes death can be seen as a blessing.

Here are some other argument points that people like to put in to prop up this theory. I am not diving too deeply into these because they are "supportive" of the Noah scripture, which, in my opinion, we have shredded.

> *Now there was a day when the sons of God came to present themselves before the Lord, and Satan also came among them.*
>
> —Job 1:6

We have *zero* Bible scripture that says angels had a "day" when they presented themselves to God. These were human men following the rules God told them to. These were *Hebrews* following their rules during one of the feasts.

> *Three times in a year all your males shall appear before the Lord **your God** in the place which He chooses, at the Feast of Unleavened Bread, the Feast of Weeks, and the Feast of Booths, and they shall not appear before the Lord empty-handed.*
>
> —Deut. 16:16

The central tent in the middle of the tribes was the house of God. Only the priests were allowed to go in there except for three times a year. During these very specific times, each man of the tribe *must* present himself to God.

Next . . .

When the morning stars sang together,
And all the sons of God shouted for joy?

—Job 38:7

These are the stars—and yes, they make noise, lots of noise. I made a campfire with my children once, and it made a lot of noise. Can you imagine what a bazillion little nuclear explosions—aka a star—sound like? This is referring to everything God created. Job 38 is an overwhelmingly poetic and accusatory chunk of scripture. Read it for yourselves.

Every good thing given and every perfect gift is from above, coming down from the Father of lights, with whom there is no variation or shifting shadow.

—James 1:17

Then God said, "Let there be lights in the expanse of the heavens to separate the day from the night, and let them be for signs and for seasons and for days and years; and let them be for lights in the expanse of the heavens to give light on the earth"; and it was so. God made the two great lights, the greater light to govern the day, and the lesser light to govern the night; He made **the stars also.**

—Gen. 1:14–16

This isn't out-of-order wording. I will explain it in another book in a chapter called "Creation." It is wild, but it follows the creation story perfectly.

But Glen, inanimate objects don't shout. Really? Is that what Jesus said?

But Jesus answered, "I tell you, if these become silent, the stones will cry out!"

—Luke 19:40

Technically, every atom on earth has electrons flying around the outside of them—and movement means *noise*. Stars create a *ton* of noise.

He is talking about the stars.

Next . . .

And angels who did not keep their own domain but abandoned their proper abode, He has kept in eternal bonds under darkness for the judgment of the great day,

—Jude 1:6

Their first estate was heaven, serving God. Now they are on earth and defiant. That is an easy one, people. C'mon!

For if God did not spare angels when they sinned, but cast them into hell and committed them to pits of darkness, reserved for judgment.

—2 Pet. 2:4

And the great dragon was thrown down, the serpent of old who is called the devil and Satan, who deceives the whole world; he was thrown down to the earth, and his angels were thrown down with him.

—Rev. 12:9

I know these say thrown down to hell . . . with a stopover on earth. Go back and look at the serpent's punishment in the

Garden of Eden. First, he is cursed to walk the earth. Think of it as sentencing a person to death. We don't do it immediately. It could take months for all the right people to be in place, but eventually, according to Revelation, everything will be in place, and the devil will get his due.

When was Satan "thrown down" to earth?

The seventy returned with joy, saying, "Lord, even the demons are subject to us in Your name." And He said to them, "I was watching Satan fall from heaven like lightning. Behold, I have given you authority to tread on serpents and scorpions, and over all the power of the enemy, and nothing will injure you. Nevertheless do not rejoice in this, that the spirits are subject to you, but rejoice that your names are recorded in heaven."

—Luke 10:17–20

How you have fallen from heaven,
O star of the morning, son of the dawn!
You have been cut down to the earth,
You who have weakened the nations!

—Isa. 14:12

You were the anointed cherub who covers,
And I placed you there.
You were on the holy mountain of God;
You walked in the midst of the stones of fire.
You were blameless in your ways,
From the day you were created Until unrighteousness was found in you.
By the abundance of your trade

You were internally filled with violence,
And you sinned;
Therefore I have cast you as profane
From the mountain of God.
And I have destroyed you, O covering cherub,
From the midst of the stones of fire.

—Ezek. 28:14–16

Satan is on earth. He and the fallen angels were sentenced to hell . . . eventually. Revelation is telling what has already happened.

The angels' original domain was heaven. Because they fought against God and rebelled, they, including Satan, were cast out and can no longer reclaim their first domain.

In my opinion, the reason the Bible addresses this angel thing so much is because even back in the days of Moses, the author of Genesis, people were trying to blame angels for what humans did.

Leave this teaching alone, people. It is bad fruit.

The last one is Peter.

For Christ also died for sins once for all, the just for the
unjust, so that He might bring us to God, having been
put to death in the flesh, but made alive in the spirit;
in which also He went and made proclamation to the
spirits now in prison, who once were disobedient when
the patience of God kept waiting in the days of Noah,
during the construction of the ark, in which a few, that
is, eight persons, were brought safely through the water.

—1 Pet. 3:18–20

Christ died, went to hell, preached to . . . not angels. In the days of Noah, God judged the *entire* world, and only Noah was found righteous. These people, these *humans*, have already faced their judgment and are, right now, in hell. Right now there are men and women in hell. Yes.

We all get turned around in the Bible from time to time, especially in the beginning when we are first stumbling through the Word. I know it can get very confusing.

I jumped on this human-angel hybrid train a long time ago, but another brother showed me the truth. In the end, the greatest argument for me *against* this teaching is a question. Did God make things to procreate only with their own kind?

Nowhere in the Bible or on earth does anyone suggest that an elephant and a gorilla can cross-breed. Neither can a giraffe and a lion or a human and anything else. Why would God get pissed if he designed our DNA to be compatible with angel DNA and then get surprised when we "played with our toys together"?

He got pissed just like any daddy gets pissed when his kid does something stupid and gets hurt time and time again. God knew humans would grow violent. He knew he would get pissed. He knew he would flood the world, and he knew he would preserve mankind through Noah. Satan and the fallen survived the flood because they are spirits and have the power of flight. Don't forget, when the world flooded, there would have been massive floating piles of trees, so even if these spirits had an earthly need to be on dry land after the flood, there would have been a way. Keep in mind that this last part (the floating trees) is *not* recorded anywhere in the Bible and is just me imagining the possibilities.

Humans on the trees theoretically would have died because of the lack of food. But angels who fell, who God cursed to walk the earth until the events in Revelation come to pass, well, that's a different story.

Also keep in mind that if the Nephilim survived on floating trees during the flood, it would have made the flood *pointless*.

My God knows exactly what he wants to do when he wants to do it and then does it, and that is the end of it.

For those who have read this and still believe in angel-human sex, I have two final thoughts. First, where is your proof in the Bible? Genesis clearly says they were here *before* the sons of God hooked up with the daughters of men. Second, your God doesn't sound all-knowing, but I will continue to pray for you.

MAN VS. WOMAN

Why is this important?

Oh, trust me. This will get really, really good.

First, we are going to talk to the boys (men).

Do you want to know why you're addicted to porn and why you are stealing glances at women? How about why you have had so many past broken relationships? I'm going to tell you why, but you're not going to believe me. I'm still going to tell you why, but first and foremost, we need to talk about Paul. He spoke from a virgin's perspective with the Holy Spirit inside of him. Since Paul was a rabbi, theoretically there is a very good chance he was being groomed to be a rabbi from a young age and didn't fall into being tempted by women. He also was not married, and I very seriously doubt he fell into the temptation of women after he came to Christ. Paul, in my *opinion*, was a virgin, spoke like a virgin, and said virgin-type things.

I am the opposite of Paul. I have been a slut. I would've said whore, but at least a whore gets paid. I just did it because I wanted to, much to my shame. I have experienced relationships, friendships, one-night hook-ups, and stress-relief friends. I've been in bad marriages and visited a prostitute. I went to four senior proms. I joined the Marine Corps and traveled the globe. Believe me, I've had a wealth of sinful knowledge regarding the female species. I have also known some very biblical women as sisters and mothers. I have more experience than Paul, my apostle, the apostle to the Gentiles. I am not saying I'm better than Paul. What I'm saying is that I have more experience with women.

I'm going to tell you some truths . . . in my opinion.

Paul's writings are scripture.

My comments are my opinion.

Paul's comments overrule mine, but don't be surprised if there are different points of view because of our different experiences—he was a virgin, and I was a slut.

But when Cephas came to Antioch, I opposed him to his face, because he stood condemned. For prior to the coming of certain men from James, he used to eat with the Gentiles; but when they came, he began to withdraw and hold himself aloof, fearing the party of the circumcision. The rest of the Jews joined him in hypocrisy, with the result that even Barnabas was carried away by their hypocrisy. But when I saw that they were not straightforward about the truth of the gospel, I said to Cephas in the presence of all, "If you, being a Jew, live like the Gentiles and not like the Jews, how is it that you compel the Gentiles to live like Jews?

We are Jews by nature and not sinners from among the Gentiles; nevertheless knowing that a man is not justified by the works of the Law but through faith in Christ Jesus, even we have believed in Christ Jesus, so that we may be justified by faith in Christ and not by the works of the Law; since by the works of the Law no flesh will be justified. But if, while seeking to be justified in Christ, we ourselves have also been found sinners, is Christ then a minister of sin? May it never be! For if I rebuild what I have once destroyed, I prove myself to be a transgressor. For through [j]the Law I died to the Law, so that I might live to God.

—Gal. 2:11–19

Just to set the scene very clearly, we have two apostles who are disagreeing. They were both servants of God. They were both tools, and they disagreed about how God was using both of those tools because they were of the mind (or at least Peter was of the mind) that Paul should look just like Peter. And Peter didn't understand that Paul was a different tool.

Jesus Christ said that in the days of Noah, so shall it be in the end, and I guarantee right here, right now, that 99.99 percent of y'all have no clue what I'm talking about.

But of that day and hour no one knows, not even the angels of heaven, nor the Son, but the Father alone. For the coming of the Son of Man will be just like the days of Noah. For as in those days before the flood they were eating and drinking, marrying and giving in marriage, until the day that Noah entered the ark, and they did not understand until the flood came and took them all away; so will the coming of the Son of Man be.

—Matt. 24:36–39

Now we are going to swing back to the Garden of Eden—specifically, our punishments.

25

To the woman He said,
"I will greatly multiply
Your pain in childbirth,
In pain you will bring forth children;
Yet your desire will be for your husband,
And he will rule over you."
Then to Adam, He said, "Because you have listened to
the voice of your wife, and have eaten from the tree about
which I commanded you, saying, 'You shall not eat from it';
Cursed is the ground because of you;
In toil you will eat of it
All the days of your life.
Both thorns and thistles it shall grow for you;
Yet you will eat the plants of the field;
By the sweat of your face
You will eat bread,
Til you return to the ground,
Because from it you were taken;
For you are dust,
And to dust you shall return."

—Gen. 3:16–19

The big kicker here is that her desire will be for her husband. America and the church will tell you to get married young. Paul says that to prevent fornication, let each man have his own wife.

But because of immoralities, each man is to have his own
wife, and each woman is to have her own husband.

—1 Cor. 7:2

America says have all the sex you want if you have a condom. You're both of age, and it's consensual.

I'm going to tell you something different. I'm talking to most young men 18 to 30-ish. In my opinion, you have no business having a girlfriend or getting married at all.

You are still figuring out how to be a man, and you're going to lead a family at 18? You're not even old enough to drink in America, and you're going to lead a family? At 25, most of you just got out of college. You have no clue what being an actual adult looks like, and you're going to lead a family? Do you want to know why there's so much divorce? Because you're not manly according to God (this does not apply to all men, so take it as it applies). What does manly look like? It's simple. Let me ask you this.

What mission are you on for God?

What is your God-filled purpose today?

What mission are you on, or are you just trying to make some money to pay off that car? Then you go to the gym, and on Sundays, you go to church. Maybe you meet with a Bible study group, or maybe you have a men's gathering at church where you discuss scripture once a week. Don't get me wrong; these are good things. But what mission are you on?

The reason I ask you this is because God gave you a helper.

Then the Lord God said, "It is not good for the man to be alone; I will make him a helper suitable for him."

—Gen. 2:18

How for the literal love of God is she supposed to help you when you have no mission? You are a cowboy still stuck in the barn. You are a tool still in the shed. You are a car still in the garage. You're of no use to a woman other than friendship in a sisterly manner, and that is what it boils down to. This is where we're going to separate the men from the boys.

If you are a man who is ready for marriage, then you should have a life that is ready to receive a helper. And I do not mean a slave—I mean a helper. I'm going to say something that is going to piss off a whole lot of you, but I don't care.

In days gone by, the value of a woman was how pretty she was. It was how good she could cook, how well she can manage the house while her husband is at work.

Right?

That is the image that *Leave It to Beaver* gave us. But let me ask you this: what is the value of a woman today?

I tell you, the value of a woman, according to the Bible, has always been that she is your helper, but if you don't have a mission, what is she going to help you with? This is one of the main reasons men step out of marriages. It is why men lean into pornography. It is why men chase after other women while they're married. It is because they are not on the mission God has for them. They are not hunting after God first. They're hunting after the flesh of this world.

Do you understand as Christians that a woman is to be treated like either your sister or your mother until God tells you this woman is to be your wife?

Do not sharply rebuke an older man, but rather appeal to him as a father, to the younger men as brothers, the older women as mothers, and the younger women as sisters, in all purity.

—1 Tim. 5:1–2

I agree that this passage is talking specifically about rebuking, but the intent is clear. Treat these people like close family.

Is that how you treat her? No.

You're going to look at your "sister" and say she's pretty.

You like the way she smells.

She makes you laugh.

She's pleasing to the eyes.

And then your boy parts start rumbling because you're worried about the pleasures of this flesh instead of being worried about the mission of God.

You fail, and you take her with you. The failing of the marriage is the man's fault every time. I do know some good men who did their best to hold their marriage together, serving God. I agree that I don't think they could have done anything better, but you're the captain of the ship. You will always bear the fault no matter what, even if it was 100 percent her fault. You will always bear the fault because you're the head of the family. The buck stops with you. Most failures in marriages that I have seen were a good percent of both people's fault.

Let me ask you something, young man.

Are you ready to be the head of the family?

Are you ready to take the responsibility of that woman on yourself?

Are you ready to be in charge?

Are you ready to not have a 50-50 relationship?

Are you ready to lead your family to God every day the way Job did?

If you don't know what I mean, I promise you, you're not ready, young man.

Could you be the one shining unicorn that defies the odds?

The situation I present here is not going to be a 100 percent fit for every male on the planet, but most men I know who are 35 and younger fall into this category.

Let me ask you this, pastors. Take a poll of all the men below 35 years old in your church, and ask them this simple question: "Do you feel like you are truly doing your calling right now?"

Most will say no. To be quite honest, a handful of 40-year-old males will also say this.

You see, boys, when you know your calling, everything else just fades into the background a little bit. Your calling pulls at you every day in a healthy way. It draws you in, but let's change gears for just a moment and discuss the fledgling state of a modern male.

I know men who have no clue how to change a diaper, no clue what their kids' teachers' names are, no clue what classes their kids are taking, and no clue how to put a meal together for their kids. I know a lot of males who come home from work and just sit and watch TV. Modern males come home and play video games. Maybe they watch a ball game, take a shower, or go to sleep.

You're not living life; you are coasting through it. Even if you have the best wife in the world, your marriage will never be what it can be with this attitude because *you* are the captain. Our example had a great wife, so now let's imagine you have an average wife, and instead of an average marriage, you have a rough marriage. The same standard still exists.

Don't believe old Glen. Let's look at some statistics. I read recently that around 80 percent of males who are married masturbate regularly. Google it, Bro.

Still, want to tell me how happy you are in your marriage, boys?

That's not even the worst statistic. The worst one is what these men are thinking while performing the act.

That's right. They're thinking about past relationships, ladies at the office, and pretty much anyone other than their spouse.

Enough of that for a minute. Let's change gears again.

Christians, are you sure that sexualizing our children and teenagers is a good idea?

Whoa! Glen, what are you talking about now?

I am talking about eighth-grade dances, proms, dating in high school, dating in college, television shows that openly have inappropriate dance sequences, skimpy "athletic" uniforms, disgusting displays of anti-biblical examples with cheerleading, girls going boy band crazy—all of it.

Dating is practicing marriage. If you as a male cannot provide for your helper, you shouldn't have one. If you aren't in the position to have one, you shouldn't practice.

Go ahead and google the percentage of Christians who divorce.

Again, men, what is your mission?

You just saw the curse handed down in the Garden of Eden. Our job is to work the land. Period. God, not your 16-year-old hormones, will add a woman to you when he sees fit, just like he did with Adam. Stop practicing marriage. Marriage for a male is about leadership—not dictatorship, not follow-ship, but leadership.

Are you ready to lead your wife every day—every single day—for the rest of your life?

In the morning, you wake up, and you're a leader. At night, whenever you go to bed, you're a leader. In the middle of the afternoon, you're a leader.

You do things to appreciate her. You recognize her hard

work, just like a leader. You make sure she feels like she's being treated fairly, as a leader does. You make sure her needs are met as a leader does.

Leadership does not mean you have to satisfy her every want and desire. It means you lead. You don't build her dreams because you are too busy working on God's will.

Let me ask you, young man, how many companies have you worked for where you as an employee told your boss what hours you were going to work; what you wanted your pay to be; what medical, dental, vision, and 401(k) plan you wanted; what company vehicle you wanted; what gas card you wanted; and anything else?

How many of y'all walked into an interview and said you wanted all these things? Did you tell them everything you wanted and that you wouldn't accept anything less?

They would probably show you the door and politely say, "Yeah, you're definitely not a candidate for this position."

But why? Why wouldn't you do that in an interview, and why wouldn't they agree to it? It's because the follower doesn't set the rules; the leader does. I am not trying to imply that your wife will be your employee, but I am making the point that as a leader you must be able to do what is best for the company (i.e., the kingdom of God) and *not* make bad deals with employees (your wife). I have just restated exactly what our punishment was in the Garden of Eden.

You have a mission. She has a job to do.

Part of your mission is to make sure she has everything she needs to complete her mission, which means you need to be knowledgeable about everything she is doing.

Paul point-blank tells women to "go home and ask your husband."

If they desire to learn anything, let them ask their own husbands at home; for it is improper for a woman to speak in church.

—1 Cor. 14:35

This means *very clearly* that you are to be knowledgeable about all things, including the Bible, so when she comes asking about things in the Bible, you might have the answers.

Your job is the mission of God. Her job is to help you, not do the work for you. Christ made the parallel extremely clear when he said that the man is the head of the wife, *exactly* like Christ is the head of the church.

Wives, be subject to your own husbands, as to the Lord. For the husband is the head of the wife, as Christ also is the head of the church, He Himself being the Savior of the body. But as the church is subject to Christ, so also the wives ought to be to their husbands in everything.

Husbands, love your wives, just as Christ also loved the church and gave Himself up for her, so that He might sanctify her, having cleansed her by the washing of water with the word,

—Eph. 5:22–26

Let me ask you this: are you treating that woman the same way Christ treated the congregation?

Or are you trying to be 50-50 equals?

Are you letting her run the family?

Are you just looking for a friend?

Young men, are you ready to stand in the fullness of Paul's

order, Christ's direction, God's curse, and your own body's design?

Are you ready to lead this family?

Why is there so much divorce, my Christian brothers? It's simple. We are not following God's orders. We are not leading. That brings ruin, and we are the captain of the ship.

Say it with me, gentleman. I want you to say it out loud, and I want you to say it proudly! It is best to devote your whole life to God but to prevent fornication, let each man have his own wife.

Come on, boys, let's say it again. Targeting the super-duper important part is that it is best to stay devoted to God!

I reckon a slut like me and a virgin like Paul just might have a similar view. Can anyone guess why?

Let me ask you this, parents. How many of you raise your sons to look at marriage as a secondary path of life, or did you tell them that one day they were going to have a wife?

One day you're going to procreate.

One day you're going to have kids.

Did you build up inside of your child this entire plan, a life plan, to finish high school, maybe go to college, get out of college, get a job for a while, find a wife, get married, and then have kids? Where in there did you put Paul's direction? I know, it can sometimes be hard to remember, so I will write it again.

It is best to stay devoted to God.

This is the failure of our parents that is manifested in us men today. Are you telling me Paul was wrong? I can justify Paul having some certain points of view issues, but can you?

To me, we have some countering to do. Or at least when you're not rightly dividing the word of truth, it looks like we have some clashing scripture.

In Genesis 1, we were told to procreate.

God blessed them; and God said to them, "Be fruitful and multiply, and fill the earth, and subdue it; and rule over the fish of the sea and over the birds of the sky and over every living thing that moves on the earth."

—Gen. 1:28

We're also told in Genesis 2 that it's not good for man to be alone.

Then the Lord God said, "It is not good for the man to be alone; I will make him a helper suitable for him."

—Gen. 2:18

Now we are seeing that it's best to serve God, but to prevent you from committing sexual sin and because you can't control yourself, then go ahead and take a woman and make her your wife.

Now concerning the things about which you wrote, it is good for a man not to touch a woman. But because of immoralities, each man is to have his own wife, and each woman is to have her own husband.

—1 Cor. 7:1–2

Paul is coming from a virgin's perspective with the Holy Spirit driving it. I'm not saying he was wrong. I'm saying he was dead-on accurate, but how can you line up this passage with the Old Testament?

I'll tell you what I believe God is telling us. Notice I used the word *believe* and not *know*.

I don't want to hear any crap about *Enough Chaos* teaching blasphemy. I'm telling you my hunch because we have what looks like clashing scripture, but from a slut-turned-Christian perspective, I'm going to try to unlock this for you.

First, when God spoke to Adam and Eve, the commission was to the entire human race. God spoke to every human on the planet—only two at that time—and said to multiply. Now we have 7.9 billion people on the planet. I think we have been doing a good job, but that is just my opinion.

Second, God gave Adam a helper *when he was on the mission from God.*

Then the Lord God formed the man of dust from the ground, and breathed into his nostrils the breath of life; and the man became a living being.

—Gen. 2:7

God makes man.

Then the Lord God took the man and put him in the Garden of Eden to cultivate it and keep it.

—Gen. 2:15

God puts man on his mission.

Then the Lord God said, "It is not good for the man to be alone; I will make him a helper suitable for him."

—Gen. 2:18

God makes Adam a helper.

Young men, get your life right with God, and then if God wants to give you a wife, he'll give you a wife, and she will be your helper. But you are to be like Christ was to the church. Was Christ a pushover, waxing, and waning as the wind blew? Was Christ a puppy following church leaders around?

You are to be over your wife, which means you must know her job. It means you must not only know male scripture but female scripture too. "Female scripture?" you may ask. Well, let me show you some—not all— of them.

Gen. 3:16	Titus 2:3	Titus 2:4	Titus 2:5
Col. 3:18	1 Pet. 3:1	1 Pet. 3:2	1 Pet. 3:3
1 Pet. 3:4	1 Tim. 2:9	1 Tim. 2:10	1 Tim. 2:11
1 Tim. 2:12	1 Tim. 2:13	1 Tim. 2:14	1 Tim. 2:15

You must learn how to be a good boss before you have your own company. You learn how to be a good boss by *following Christ*, reading the Bible, praying, talking to sound biblical men/elders, tuning in to the Holy Spirit, and doing your best not to grieve him. Talk to God. Hunger after God. Thirst after God, and when you are on your mission from God, if it is His will, you will be given a helper to multiply your mission.

Here are some things to remember:

Don't take "it" when you want to give "it."
Don't assume that your wife will wash your clothes.
Don't make her rub your back.
She doesn't have to always make dinner.
She's not your trophy wife.

If she does these things to help you focus better on the mission, then that's okay. Maybe it is the role God wants for her, but when she's over there cooking, cleaning, and taking care of the kids and you're sitting there watching the ball game, you have failed, Mr. Spiritual Leader of the family. Christ never sat there and watched a baseball game when all the apostles were working.

Show me your little sports games or your car clubs in the Bible. Show me where Scripture tells us to run away into man caves, video games, sports, cars, movies, and all other forms of entertainment.

I'm not saying these things are bad, but I'm asking you to think about how much time you devote to your hobbies compared to how much time you devote to the mission of God.

I'm not talking about learning more about God. I'm not talking about going to church on Sundays to hear the sermon because that's just a normal baseline event.

I'm talking about the mission God has given you, specifically *you*. Is it running an orphanage? Is it volunteering at an animal shelter? Is it building little old ladies' fences? What mission are you on for God? Is it teaching? *What are you doing for the kingdom?* If you have no mission, you have no need of a woman to be a helper. The world is being populated wholesale. That mandate is being achieved. As for it not being good that man is alone, I have a family, a cell phone, social media, and a handful of close friends. By the way, I have the Holy Spirit too—just saying. My personal belief is that you can never truly deserve a helper because you are covered in sin, but we should still try our best to earn her.

A helper is not a servant, a slave, a maid, or a cook. And just between us, do you want a woman to serve you food? We saw what happened to Adam when Eve served him a meal. *(Haha!*

That was absolutely a joke for those of you with no sense of humor. Don't worry; it won't happen again . . . maybe.)

So here is the summation.

Throw all women in terms of intimacy boyfriend-girlfriend dating out the window. Stop thirsting after a wife.

"But a man has needs," you might say.

What did Christ say about your needs? I believe he said if your hand causes you to sin, cut it off. Right?

Now if your right eye makes you stumble, tear it out and throw it from you; for it is better for you to lose one of the parts of your body, than for your whole body to be thrown into hell. If your right hand makes you stumble, cut it off and throw it from you; for it is better for you to lose one of the parts of your body, than for your whole body to go into hell.

—Matt. 5:29–30

Oh yeah, you know exactly what I'm talking about, and I know exactly what you're thinking about. And we both know exactly what Christ was *directly* talking about.

Now you need to make this right with Jesus Christ, your Lord, and Savior. Admit to Christ that you can't control your actions, you can't control your body, and you want to blame it on God for giving you these needs instead of blaming it on yourself for your lack of discipline and your lack of faith in God.

Your wee-wee is to be used for urination unless God himself brings you an earthly wife, and if you can't keep your hand off of it, cut that hand off.

Rushing God or rushing this woman is only going to end in failure or an unhappy marriage. It might even end in both of you turning gray (lukewarm) and then hell.

*So because you are lukewarm, and neither hot nor cold, I
will spit you out of My mouth.*

—Rev. 3:16

Remember . . . God's timing, not mine. God's opinion, not
mine.

God's love shows me how to love, and once I have raised
myself up to the Holy Spirit through scripture, meditation,
and prayer, we can find comfort in the storm.

I need sound doctrine through fellowship with other men.

I need sound doctrine through reading the Good Book
myself.

I need godly elders to help me along my path.

Maybe God will bring a woman into my life to help me on
my ministry, or maybe not.

*If it be so, our God whom we serve is able to rescue us
from the furnace of blazing fire; and He will deliver us
out of your hand, O king. But even if He does not, let it
be known to you, O king, that we are not going to serve
your gods or worship the golden statue that you have
set up.*

—Dan. 3:17–18

If you don't have a mission, why do you have a wife? Why
do you need a helper? Is it so you can build a better building?
Is it so that you can work at a gas station? Is it so you can
sell electronics at Best Buy? I'm not saying these are bad jobs.
What I am saying very clearly is that these are your earthly
kingdom things. Do you think that's why God gave you your
wife?

It's in the Bible. It says it's not good for man to be alone, so we made him a helpmate . . . when Adam was on the mission God had assigned him. Your godly mission could be doing something earthly, but there will be no doubt that you are on your mission. There will be a wholeness that fills your veins. And *if* God wants you to have help, he will give you a helper.

Again, do you want to know why there's so much divorce in the Christian faith? It's because most men have no clue what their mission is, and they get married and drag their wife down this aimless, pointless rat race of life. Her desire is for her husband, but he doesn't have a clue what he's doing because he didn't take the time to grow up in the faith, stand strong, and learn how to lead. He just jumped into marriage and said oh well, we'll just wing it and hope for the best, and somewhere along the journey, he started obeying her or ignoring her.

> *Then to Adam, He said, "Because you have listened to the voice of your wife, and have eaten from the tree about which I commanded you, saying, 'You shall not eat from it'; Cursed is the ground because of you; In toil you will eat of it All the days of your life."*

> —Gen. 3:17

Gentlemen, I'm going to give you the line of questioning you might want to ask yourself before getting in a relationship.

1. Am I ready to lead a family the way Christ led the church?

2. Am I "on mission"?

41

If the answers to these questions are yes, then it's time for her to answer some questions. (If the answers are no, then get back to work.)

Look her dead in the eye, and ask, "What are you going to help me with?"

And when she says, "I'm going to cook for you," you might want to say that you can cook for yourself. Then ask what else she is going to do.

When she says, "I'm going to make babies with you," I recommend saying you can adopt children on your own. Then ask, "What else have you got?"

When she says, "I'm going to keep the house clean for you," I recommend saying that you can hire a maid.

And when she says, "I am going to help you prevent fornication," I recommend saying you are a disciplined man who is devoted to God, and that is not an issue.

I cannot give you the right answer to the question, and I'm sorry for that, my brothers.

What I can do is tell you some of the wrong answers. I don't know your specific mission, so I don't know how God is pulling this woman in to help you on your mission. That is assuming it is God pulling this woman in and not just the pleasures of the flesh.

I will give you a critical piece of advice, though. You don't want a woman who thinks her only value is cooking, cleaning, and making babies. That is not a biblical woman. A biblical woman may have those qualities as bonuses, but that is not her prime directive—her purpose in life.

No, my friend, her prime directive is the same as yours. Love God. Serve God. And then be a helper after that. If she doesn't already know that when you're having this conversation, then my advice is simple: run. Run like hell is chasing you.

In my opinion, the reason Christian marriages are trashed in this country is simple. Men keep marrying to fulfill manmade life progression points or because they yearn for the pleasures of the flesh.

If you men (me too) *stop* getting married until you are "on mission," you will see a difference.

If we start treating our wives like Christ treated the church (instead of treating her like Christ treated God with admiration, reverence, and worship), I have a strong hunch we will stop seeing so many women with a hyperinflated sense of self (that every woman is a queen, everything about them is wonderful, and there is nothing wrong with them). None of these confidence-boosting thoughts are biblical, not even one of them. These are literal statements that go against the Bible and tell everyone that they are a product of the world, not Christ.

Men, this is our fault. We are the heads of the family, and we have stopped leading our wives. We have failed to correct them with love the way God corrected the church. Even Paul corrected the church, but we seldom call our wives down for committing open and repeated sins. Why do we not call them out? It's simple. We, the leaders, are selling the company down the river so we can have a friend. We are agreeing to eat the forbidden fruit so we won't be alone. We have displayed gross negligence and open rebellion. *We are the problem.*

I for one will never again be the problem. I am doing my best to remove all sin I possibly can from my life. I am doing my best to lean on God in every way I possibly can. I stopped asking for a helper. I had two and failed them both. I don't know if I can take another one, boys. I will obey God . . . but I am terrified of going through the gut-wrenching process of divorce again. Give me a war zone. Give me a million yards of fence to install with a broken hammer. Give me an Excel spreadsheet that is always bugged. Give me a mission to tell every man on earth that we all suck really, really badly. Make me watch *Carrot Top* reruns for five years straight. I fear none of these. I fear having another helper, though.

It is best to stay single and devoted to God, especially in modern days. Stay on mission, boys. The end is nigh.

For the Ladies

Oh, my sisters, guess what? It's ladies' night at *Enough Chaos*, and if you didn't like the McDonald's burger I just served to the men, buckle up, females, because this is about to turn into a banquet.

Women, most of y'all are going to hate me after this one, but that's okay. I have two ex-wives who already hate me and a mother who tried to kill me when I was 12. I promise you, there ain't nothing you can say that one of my ex-wives or my mother hasn't said to me first, so bring it on, baby girl.

I'm going to preface this next part by saying I'm *not* talking to or about *all women*. I even emphasized those words, so when I get hate from a woman who doesn't fall in the category I lay out, I can easily refer them back to those words. But there is a large group of women I am talking to specifically—women in the church.

If my words or tone make you feel a little uncomfortable, I'm not talking to you right now.

If my words kind of rile you up a little bit, I'm probably not talking to you—probably.

But if my words sting you, I am absolutely 100 percent talking to you.

If my words offend you, then you are my target, and I don't care. I just took on all-male Christians who historically have waged war on the planet and committed atrocities against the weak, the simple-minded, and the poor. Bring it on, kitty cat. I was not put on this earth to play nursemaid to your feelings. I don't care if you hate me. I have some truths to give you. It is up to you to open the box.

The group of women I'm talking to is my "equality" women—the women who claim to be Christians and want equality with men.

All right, ladies, you make up 53 percent of the population in America.

I say we initiate a military draft until you also make up 53 percent of the armed forces in every occupation, including combat. Get ready to start having more of your daughters, mothers, and sisters come back in body bags and miles and miles of PTSD (post-traumatic stress disorder) because it's high time the males of this country stop protecting you. Equality, right?

Then I say we fire male cops until we have female-male equality for the numbers. Every time a female cop is fired, a male cop gets fired too. Every time a male cop is hired so does a female cop. If we can't find enough female cops, we just let the city burn.

I like this equality thing. Go big or go home, right?

Why don't we apply that to every nasty, tough, rough job such as farming, welding, roofing, and plumbing? How about waste management? If we can't find enough females to fill 53 percent of the nasty and back-breaking jobs males have always filled, who cares as long as it is fair? Let the city fall apart.

For every occupation in this country, women must occupy 53 percent of the spots.

I agree with you, ladies. I want you women and only you women specifically to be treated exactly like a man in every way.

From now on in divorce court, the judge does not get to see the man and the woman in court. Their lawyers will represent the case to the judge 100 percent. There will be no use of the words *he* or *she*, and there will be no using their names. From now on in divorce court, people will only be known by their birthdates—not the year because men tend to be older but just the month and day. From now on we're going to let the facts of who's the better parent get custody of the kids instead of the woman always getting it. That's fair, right?

Do you want equality? Come on, birthing parent, walk down the road with me. From now on there are no more separate men's and women's drunk tanks. All jails and prisons across the land should be co-ed. That way you women can get just as assaulted as the men do while the guards aren't looking. Granted, statistics say that a female in prison is twice as likely to be sexually assaulted by a female as a male in a male prison. But let's keep in mind some facts. First, how many men are not reporting the rape? Second, what do you think this will look like when we go co-ed?

Equality, right? Each tank must contain 53 percent females.

Feel free to go to your favorite Internet search engine and type in transgender MMA fighter versus female. Your desire for equality is already starting to creep in, but to make you happy, we should probably go a step further.

From now on, there is *zero* male or female sports in pre-K or elementary school, middle school, high school, college, adult sports, MMA, boxing, and the Olympics. Female basketball has always struggled to stay alive, but how do you think that is going to go with males mixed in? Female softball? Not anymore All teams must have 47 percent males on each team. Females probably do have an advantage in diving competitions regarding small splashes, but we have a problem. Most sports doctors would agree that men have a distinct advantage over females in sports, but none of that matters now because we will be equals.

Equality smells good, doesn't it?

From now on, when females do something that medically takes them out of the labor force, they will be treated exactly like a man who works construction and breaks his foot on his personal time. He will most likely be fired because they are no longer able to fulfill the job description. I'm sure a handful of you are scratching your heads inquisitively. Think about it, birthing parent.

Let's look at females in the military. Let's look at females in the military right before their unit deploys. Oh yeah. There's the destruction of military property because you didn't have the right to get pregnant. It's just like if a male in the military accidentally cuts off their dad-gum leg on personal time. The military could press charges on you for the destruction of government property.

Do you know how many women I've heard of and know personally who got out of deployment because they were pregnant?

Do you want equality? You're about to get it, ma'am.

By the way, I saw a study that said 57 percent of college students are female. That's not fair. Get those girls packing and send them back home. Females can only make up 53 percent of the college population. Every high school graduating class *must* be 53 percent female. Get ready to deny some graduations, ladies.

All of those office-working females had better get some construction boots because from now on, only 53 percent of your office workers can be female.

School teachers – 53 percent.
Medical personnel – 53 percent.

The list of mandatory job reassignments will be a mile long, but you ladies will surely get your freedom from the oppressive men who hold you back.

You ladies know the female-only gyms. Well, those aren't fair. They are gone.

Sports attire—unisex sports attire is mandatory, *exactly* the same uniform for males and females. That applies to sports, military, law enforcement, medical, schools, and anywhere a uniform is mandatory. (P.S. I hate places like Hooters, so this would be a massive improvement.)

As I promised you, I have teeth, and I bite back. When I bite back, I go for the throat.

If you want equality, then stand up and take it for yourself, and stop asking other people to give it to you.

When you ask somebody for equality and expect the answer to be yes, it's called entitlement. When a man wants equality, he betters himself and strives for a better run-time, a better academic foundation, and better power tools. When a man wants equality, he doesn't kick and cry; he just hammers the nail down until he achieves his goal. When you stand up and take your equality, that is true freedom. As a Christian, when you want equality, ask yourself this: was Christ treated fairly? But you're better than that man, huh?

You know better. You can do it better. You are smarter and better in every way.

It's like when you ladies stood up and remade *Ghostbusters*.

It completely flopped because it was a horrible movie, and you tried to make it stand up on feminism and male shaming. That is what freedom looks like with equality.

Or it's like when you took the remake of *He-Man* by Netflix and made it a woman-empowerment show instead of what it originally was. It flopped, and Netflix had to release another complete relaunch of it two months later. That is what your freedom looks like with equality. By the way, this happened in 2021.

Or better yet, how about *Star Wars* when you took a female lead and make her have absolutely no character arc. Then suddenly she's teaching the best pilot in the universe how to repair his ship. She's teaching the best *Star Wars* wizard how to be a wizard. She is the greatest thing that happened to the universe, but in real life, her toys lined the shelves of stores and just couldn't sell because the character was completely unrelatable to its original massive, money-spending audience. That is your freedom with equality.

Let me ask you something. How in the world does 53 percent of the population remain subservient to the male 46 percent?

No, I didn't do the math wrong. I just threw 1 percent in there for people who are confused about what gender they are.

You females are the voting majority in America.

You are literally in control of the country.

Or is this whole feminism-equality thing just another way for you to do what God said not to do in the Garden of Eden? Is this another way for females to yet again use their God-given talents of relationship to try to mandate, browbeat, and guilt males into submission?

It didn't work in the Garden of Eden because God got mad. It didn't work in Noah's time because God got mad. Good luck making it work this time. I'm sure that won't bring about the end of the world, right?

1 Timothy 2:12 anybody?

But I do not allow a woman to teach or exercise authority over a man, but to remain quiet.

While you're stomping your feet in righteous indignation, I want you to keep one tiny little fact in the back of your mind. Hold these next words in your thoughts while you play little miss victim. Let these words burn within your soul and feed your fiery wrath for eternity.

Keep in mind that you're talking to a man who was raped by a 32-year-old woman when he was 11 years old.

Keep in mind that I was almost killed at the age of 12 by the woman who birthed me because she had stayed up all night drinking with her buddies. In the mornings, she liked a bloody Mary.

You're talking to a man who sacrificed as much as he possibly could for his family for 12 years, including going to an active war zone, line of duty shootings, and prison riots, all the while being the best possible Bible teacher to his kids that he could while he was home, often doing arts and crafts projects with his kids and being the best husband, he knew how to be. Now he only gets to see his kids four days a month. There are no more snuggles at night, no more Daddy-I'm-scared conversations at 1:00 a.m.

And what was written on that divorce certificate? Well, I can tell you it certainly wasn't the biblical mandate from Jesus Christ, which is unfaithfulness and infidelity (Matt. 19:8–9).

So come on and talk to me, little lady. Tell me specifically how the big bad men have persecuted you. Tell me how men have personally held you down. Tell me about the crimes men have committed that oppressed you. Tell me about your version of equality.

Was it equality when my mom never went to jail as she should have even though the cops took my statement? I guess attempted murder is okay when you're a woman, but let a man do it, and prison is guaranteed.

How about my rapist never going to prison as she should have? Nobody even called the cops because the victim was a male, and she was a female. Is that your equality?

Is it equal that the state of Texas decided that four days a month was all the daddy-time my children needed? Don't get me wrong. I was a crappy leader of the family, and my wife was a crappy follower, but seriously, four days a month? I am not a unicorn here. This is the "standard deal," or so my female lawyer told me.

Now that I think back on it, where was the group of people who should have surrounded us? Where were the church and the family who was supposed to come around us and talk sense into us? They were nowhere, at least regarding the man. They rallied around the woman. Is that equality to you? This situation is played out hundreds of times a day in this country. Don't believe just me. Go ask the divorced males of your Christian congregation if they felt embraced, supported, or even loved by the congregation during their divorce. Or are we always wrong because we are men?

And Little Miss Equal, do you want to know why none of these things happened?

It's because men are expected to be able to take more and never complain.

The cold, hard truth that men *know* is that nobody,

especially women, cares about our problems. Granted, there are a few women who do care, and I will talk about them later, but not women in general, not a woman who only sees what she doesn't have instead of seeing what she can give to others.

When the wolf is at the door, men are expected to grab the axe and go kill the wolf, but then women turn around and put us down for these aggressive tendencies, the traits that are required to be able to commit this act of violence to protect them. You women who are in control of this country expect men to act like women unless you want them to act like men in that single moment. But then they need to go back to being like women. Keep in mind that 343 New York firefighters died responding to the September 11, 2001 (9/11) attack. How many of them do you think were female? That wasn't fair.

When the 12 tribes of Israel came back from war, the men had to sit in a camp for seven days outside the city to be purified. Every soldier who's been in war, every cop who's been in a line of duty shooting, every firefighter who has had a brother or sister go down, every emergency room doctor and nurse who had a full moon kind of night know exactly why those soldiers had to stay out of the city for seven days.

They stayed out there because war takes a toll on your heart, and you need to civilize yourself. But you women want us, men, to fight wars and then be ready for tea and crumpets the next morning.

Christ told us to sell our cloak and buy a sword (Luke 22:36). I have heard many times that war is unchristian, that defending our home is unchristian, or that committing violence is unchristian. I'm sorry to be the bearer of bad news, but those who say that do not *know* the Christ, God, and Holy

Spirit spoken of in the Bible. You may know some other God but certainly not my God.

God flooded the world, killing almost every living creature.

Then the LORD said, "I will blot out man whom I have created from the face of the land, from man to animals to creeping things and to birds of the sky; for I am sorry that I have made them."

—Gen. 6:7

My Christ beat people in the temple with a whip in the second chapter of John.

And He found in the temple those who were selling oxen and sheep and doves, and the money changers seated at their tables. And He made a scourge of cords, and drove them all out of the temple, with the sheep and the oxen; and He poured out the coins of the money changers and overturned their tables; and to those who were selling the doves He said, "Take these things away; stop making My Father's house a place of business."

—John 2:14–16

The Holy Spirit flat out killed a liar in Acts.

But a man named Ananias, with his wife Sapphira, sold a piece of property, and kept back some of the price for himself, with his wife's full knowledge, and bringing a portion of it, he laid it at the apostles' feet. But Peter said, "Annanias, why has Satan filled your heart to lie to the Holy Spirit and to keep back some of the price of the land? While it remained unsold, did it not remain your own? And after it was sold, was it not under your control? Why is it that you have conceived this deed in your heart? You have not lied to men, but to God." And as he heard these words, Ananias fell down and breathed his last; and great fear came over all who heard of it.

—Acts 5:1–5

I am not saying we should go looking for a fight, and I am not embracing the Crusades or the trash cross-burning from our country's past. What I believe Christ was talking about was when the wolf comes to the door, the man who oversees his family is to grab the sword and cut that dad-gum wolf's head off. Men were made for a purpose, for work. Women were made for relationship.

And you women want men to be both purposeful and relational, just like you want to be both purposeful and relational, and that's why we have an entire country that has decided there are no longer male and female genders. Now you can be whatever gender you want to be.

I ask you, ladies, again, who is in control of this country? Who was the voting majority after World War II? Who was the voting majority after the Vietnam War, the Korean War, the Gulf War, Afghanistan, and Iraq?

And you tell me you want equality. Nobody cares about men, and men know it deep down in their hearts. They know no one cares about their problems.

If that's not the truth, then you tell me how many women's shelters are in your city. Now tell me how many men's shelters are in your city—not halfway houses for people getting out of prison but true shelters like women have shelters.

Go on, take out your phone, and go to your favorite search engine. Then type in "women's shelter near me." If you're in a city, write down how many are within 10 miles of you. Now type in "men's shelter near me."

Men account for up to 70 percent of the homeless population. According to my research, there are five women's shelters within 10 miles of me and only one for men.

Tell me about how unfair things are for you ladies. You see, men know you don't care. The proof is everywhere we look. But that is the problem; men know that nobody cares.

Tell me, Miss Voting Majority who are literally in control of the country. Tell me how fair divorce judges are.

I promise you that you don't want equality; you want flowers on Valentine's Day and your meals paid for and doors opened up for you, and for men to care when you're crying about nothing. I am being 100 percent literal; I have held a woman who was crying, and she had no clue why she was crying. You want all of this and more money and control of the kids and . . . and . . . and . . .

You want control, just like Eve did. But the crazy thing is that even with control like women have right now, you still aren't happy. You are the voting majority, and you still aren't happy.

And now here's the question. Why do you want control?

As in the days of Noah, so shall it be at the end.

For the coming of the Son of Man will be just like the days of Noah.

—Matt. 24:37

You want control because you're drifting away from God. Ladies, if you look around and ask where all the good men have gone, I want you to go on a search engine and research MGTOW, or Red Pill Movement. That is where a lot of them have gone, even if they don't realize that's where they've gone.

They have run into video games and pornography and fantasy football, and mainly away from you.

For the coming of the Son of Man will be just like the days of Noah.

—Matt. 24:37

That the sons of God saw that the daughters of men were beautiful; and they took wives for themselves, whomever they chose.

—Gen. 6:2

Then Noah's flood happened.

In the previous chapter of this book, we destroyed the Greek-god Zeus idea of heavenly hosts having sex with human beings and creating offspring (Hercules).

So now that I've taken everything that Satan and the darkness have done to try to muddy things up and thrown that out the window, let's look at these verses with clean eyes.

Here's my interpretation.

When Noah's sons looked around and realized there were no more godly women on the earth, they took wives from the heathen tribes. They were not godly women, but they weren't pains in the butt. They were soft, warm, and nurturing—you know, feminine. Their feminine traits bolstered the men's manly traits, and men felt like *men* around these women.

That the sons of God saw that the daughters of men were beautiful; and they took wives for themselves, whomever they chose.

—Gen. 6:2

Then God rained judgment down on the earth and killed everybody except Noah, his wife, their sons, and their wives. The ladies got in as freebies just like the sons got in as freebies because of Noah's righteousness.

These are the records of the generations of Noah. Noah was a righteous man, blameless in his time; Noah walked with God.

—Gen. 6:9

Two of his sons ended up serving God. One did not.

My strong hunch is that when Christ says it will be in the end days just as it was in the days of Noah, it is twofold.

First, look above and below the text I quoted.

For the coming of the Son of Man will be just like the days of Noah. For as in those days before the flood they were eating and drinking, marrying and giving in marriage, until the day that Noah entered the ark, and they did not understand until the flood came and took them all away; so will the coming of the Son of Man be.

—Matt. 24:37–39

It is abundantly clear that Christ is talking about how sudden his return will be, but Christ often had double or triple meanings to his words. I believe if we look at what happened that led up to the event (Noah's sons) instead of looking immediately before (Christ's reference to Noah), we can unlock the truth. There will be no more godly women on the earth, but this time there is Revelation, and the entire earth will be atoned.

Women, I've already gone after all the men. And now I've gone after some of you. Even if you don't hate me, I'm sure the men do because they have the word *guardian* written on their hearts.

Isn't that silly? Those stupid, knuckle-dragging, good-for-nothing, lazy men still want to defend you. Men are so silly and so easily manipulated by *a woman designed by God for relationship*. You are using your God-given superpower and abusing it wildly, often bragging on TikTok, Facebook, and all other forms of social media about how crafty you are. At a minimum, you brag to your closest friend(s) over wine and drinks.

One of my wives came back from a women's Christian retreat all lit up with excitement. I asked her what happened. She said she finally understood how the man is supposed to be the head of the family, and I was like oh, okay. I wanted to get some popcorn and sit down. I wanted to enjoy this. She's going to give me a revelation, right?

The words that came out of her mouth were that "the husband is the head, but the wife is the neck, and the head can't look at anything unless the neck tells it to."

This is the trash garbage my wife came home with from a Christian women's retreat. A Christian *women's retreat* taught her this nonsense.

Here's what the Bible teaches us:

Wives, be subject to your husbands, as is fitting in the Lord.

—Col. 3:18

Wives, be subject to your own husbands, as to the Lord. For the husband is the head of the wife, as Christ also is the head of the church, He Himself being the Savior of the body.

—Eph. 5:22–23

Could you imagine saying "Christ is the head of the church, but he can't do anything unless the church tells him to"?

So you Christian women can continue making fun of your men, belittling your men, gossiping behind their backs, daydreaming of living other women's lives, imagining having other men, having your little trash retreats, and passing all this garbage on to the next women coming up, but I won't stand by you.

And what you're seeing is a large group of men who don't want to stand by you either—not in public, not in relationships, not in church, not before God.

So as it was in the days of Noah, so shall it be in the end.

That the sons of God saw that the daughters of men were beautiful; and they took wives for themselves, whomever they chose.

—Gen. 6:2

Why do you think females typically outnumber males in church? That percentage is only going to get worse for

Christians. Men are starting to prefer dating outside the church rather than in the church for a reason. Don't believe me. Look at the facts yourself, and then look at yourself and ask where, oh Lord, have all the good men gone?

Do you want to know why God doesn't answer you, why all you hear is silence? It's because you did not do exactly what Paul told you to do—serve God first. Your first priority is Jesus Christ. Your first priority is to God.

But let me guess. You want that 6-foot man with a six-pack who makes six figures, has a good education, dresses mighty fine, and likes your family and friends. He can put up with being number five in your life because your kids come first, then your parents, then your friends, then your job, and then the marriage. And by the way, he does need to love your cat, too, and why, with all this going on, can't he ever seem to find time to buy you flowers?

Lord, oh Lord, where have all the good men gone?

That the sons of God saw that the daughters of men were beautiful; and they took wives for themselves, whomever they chose.

—Gen. 6:2

There are very few of us left, and many of us don't want anything to do with you because you don't make us feel like men. You don't make us feel like your man. You bring more drama into the relationship than you bring helpfulness.

Your title in the marriage is not head; it is helper. How are you helping me serve God on my mission? Don't get me wrong, ladies. The majority of men I know are *not* fit to be leaders. This is my factual opinion. They are still too consumed with childish things to be a good leader, but why are you trying to wrangle a 6-foot man-child? Find a real man of God before you say "I do." Throw all those worldly expectations of a man out with tonight's garbage, and make a biblical checklist of what a real man of God looks like. If you are already married, the Bible is clear on what you are to do.

Do you want to know where all the good men have gone? We want to know where all the good women are. Do you think maybe there's a secret island in the middle of the Atlantic that they're all gathering on?

Or maybe, just maybe, we're supposed to get right with God first and then come together in marriage later.

What does a 20-year-old girl know about herself that justifies her being able to make a lifelong commitment to help a man on his mission from God? Back in the old days when there were arranged marriages, it might have been possible because parents weren't looking through lustful eyes. They were (hopefully) looking through is-this-man-serving-God eyes. I'm not saying that's the way it should be because most parents don't genuinely have the best interest of their children in mind. That's why they push kids harder in college or sports than they ever pushed them about the Bible, God, and heaven.

What I am saying is that today as a young 20-year-old lady, you have absolutely no business choosing a man because you are looking through lustful eyes. He's pretty. He makes me smile. He makes me feel special. He has a good job. Yeah, nowhere in there was he is on a mission, he's right with God, I'm right with God and God has told me to be his wife.

And I'm sorry to say that most single 30-year-old women are also there.

And most single 40-year-old women have souls that are so calloused that being in a relationship with a man is like sandpaper that wears a man with "I require this," and "these are my needs," and "I want my own way," and—my favorite—"let me make this clear" statements.

I also know a lot of 50-year-old+ women who already have their men cowed down properly underneath their feet with that honey-do list because they're not woman enough to do it themselves. Thankfully, they have a servant to do their bidding. Good boy. I'll give you a treat tomorrow. Maybe I'll take you out for a special dinner.

I know a 60-year-old woman. Her husband drives her to the department store, parks the car, and sits in it for an hour or two while she shops. Then he comes back and picks her up. He does the same thing at the grocery store. She's got a little chauffeur. Isn't that cute?

Most women I know don't want a real man, a biblical man, a godly man. They don't want a warrior for God or a builder who could build a boat and lockout the entire world other than the eight people God said should be on that boat, literally letting the rest of the world drown. You don't want a biblical man; you want a girl in a man's body. You want a gossip buddy you can snuggle with. You want a man to stand next to you who other women desire so you can feel like you have worth.

And he just wants you to act like you like him, so he sells both of you down the river because he won't lead.

So both of you defy God with your marriage, and the world gets worse.

That's equality. Do you want a battle of the sexes? Well, ladies, you're seeing it play out.

Now let's talk about my second group of women—the females who know they are females and want to be a female according to God's Word. Some of you have had to go into the workforce. For my school teachers, my social workers, my childcare workers, any medical females, my EMT females, I thank you with all my heart for what you do every day for this country, for your state, for your county, for your city, for your church, and your home. I thank you with all my heart for nurturing us, especially when we don't deserve it. Thank you.

My third group of women is my rough girls. You are women but a special breed of women. You love God with all your heart and know your role as a female, but you are currently working in the workforce in what is considered a male job—the back-breaking, dangerous jobs. My female prison guards (yeah, I had two of you who were bad mamas, and I wanted you to have my back any time of day), my female soldiers, my female cops, my female firefighters, my female ER nurses, my female ER doctors, and the hundreds of other jobs that go into this rough category, you know who you are, and I'll buy you a beer any day, Mama. Thank you for stepping up where men should have. Thank you for suiting up with the men and putting yourself in harm's way to make the world a better place. Thank you, my battle angels, thank you. May the Lord keep you safe from harm for another day.

My fourth and final group of women are my biblical sisters and mothers who cling to the Word of God and love their men (if God has given them one). This group includes all the women from groups two and three.

My sisters and mothers, I am so sorry the country has gotten to this point. I'm sorry our men are not the men they should be, and I'm sorry the other women are not the women they should be. I've done my best as just one man serving God to be the best tool in God's hands as I can be, but I need more from you. I beg to have more from you. I plead to have more from you. I will do my best to help men become strong men of God, but ladies of the faith, please understand that if y'all fall, we all face the anger of God.

> *For our struggle is not against flesh and blood, but against the rulers, against the powers, against the world forces of this darkness, against the spiritual forces of wickedness in the heavenly places. Therefore, take up the full armor of God, so that you will be able to resist on the evil day, and having done everything, to stand firm. Stand firm therefore, having girded your loins with truth, and having put on the breastplate of righteousness, and having shod your feet with the preparation of the gospel of peace; in addition to all, taking up the shield of faith with which you will be able to extinguish all the flaming arrows of the evil one. And take the helmet of salvation, and the sword of the Spirit, which is the word of God.*

> *With all prayer and petition pray at all times in the Spirit, and with this in view, be alert with all perseverance and petition for all the saints, and pray in my behalf, that utterance may be given to me in the opening of my mouth, to make known with boldness the mystery of the gospel, for which I am an ambassador in chains; that in proclaiming it I may speak boldly, as I ought to speak.*

> —Eph. 6:12–20

Be those biblical women, for if you are lost, so is this earth until Jesus Christ comes down, and then it's pure warfare and God's anger. You ladies, as much as every man that I know would like to take this mantle from you, you are the gatekeeper to the book of Revelation, *if my opinion is true.*

You must stand.

You must use that 53 percent majority vote that you have and let your voice be heard across the country. We need you now more than ever. That little boy who got raped and nobody cared, he needed you. The little boy who had to fight off his mother as she drunkenly came after him with a barber's razor knife, he needed you. That man who came back from war zones and prison riots, he needed you. That man who had his entire world ripped away from him by a Texas judge, he needed you. That man who is left over, he doesn't need you anymore, but there are men out there who still do.

You must stand, or we will all fall. But I've got great news. You won't stand alone. If you are a biblical woman, the one true God has your back. When I ask you to stand, I am not asking you to march on Washington, DC. I am not requesting you to stand in picket lines. I am begging you to stand as lighthouses for younger women. Guide them. Teach them. And yes, ma'am, dare to reprove them with love. Call them out, and correct them.

Why do you think I wrote this "Man vs. Woman" chapter after the angel sex chapter?

The world will try to do everything it can to shadow the truth. The crystal-clear truth of the Bible is that Christian men looked at non-Christian women, saw that they were beautiful, and took them as their wives. *(Obviously, Christians were not a thing back then, but I used the new term on the old formula for clarity.)*

According to God, women are to respect (or submit to, depending on the translation) their husbands. Their desire should be for their husbands according to the Garden of Eden curse.

Modern women have no desire for their husbands. Prove that in your church, and ask all the women in your church if they have a "desire" for their husband? Have them fill out an anonymous voting thing. Then ask the men to do a separate secret vote that asks them if they feel desired by their wives. "Do you feel respected by your wife?" "Does your wife help you on your mission from God?" "Does she bring more drama into your life or helpfulness?"

Can you guess how many men I have talked to who haven't had relations with their wife in weeks, months, or even years? I ran a care ministry for two and a half years, and that short time was eye-opening for my view of modern Christian women.

Modern women have very little respect for their husbands. The volume of male-based jokes that come out of women's mouths is offensive. So is the gossiping, the backstabbing, and the belittling.

Yes, ma'am. Christian men will be abandoning the disrespectful and undesiring women of American Christian culture for other cultures' women, like Noah's sons did.

Or Christian men will abandon God, listen to their wives, and be filled with war.

That the sons of God saw that the daughters of men were beautiful; and they took wives for themselves, whomever they chose. Then the Lord said, "My Spirit shall not strive with man forever, because he also is flesh; nevertheless his days shall be one hundred and twenty years." The Nephilim were on the earth in those days, and also afterward when the sons of God came into the daughters of men, and they bore children to them. Those were the mighty men who were of old, men of renown.

Then the Lord saw that the wickedness of man was great on the earth, and that every intent of the thoughts of his heart was only evil continually. The Lord was sorry that He had made man on the earth, and He was grieved in His heart. The Lord said, "I will blot out man whom I have created from the face of the land, from man to animals to creeping things and to birds of the sky; for I am sorry that I have made them."

—Gen. 6:2–7

Just look at the Bible. It is step by step by step. The absence of biblical women brings about war, which brings about God throwing the game table over.

The next generation of males, or maybe the next after that, will revolt against everything because they have been treated so horribly. That is what happened in the days of Noah; that is what happened in my childhood, and it will happen again.

The men have failed my Ladies of the Cross. We have failed you. We failed to keep the wolf out, and now it is inside the house of God. Every time we go to cut its head off, the family stops us, but the wolf is slowly consuming our home. We, the true men of God, need your help. Please help us clean up this house. Please.

Moving on . . .

Although I nailed two specific groups of men and only one very small specific group of women, I can understand how it feels, like I pulled a flamethrower out on every person on earth. Trust me, I get it, so let me make this extremely clear.

Boys, boys, boys . . .

In the Marine Corps, we had a thing called a poop sandwich. A poop sandwich was when you put a little cream filling in the middle, but the top biscuit was poop, and the bottom biscuit was poop. Thus, it is a poop sandwich. Many people will look at this chapter and say, "Man, this was a poop sandwich He sure is crazy with the women, but he didn't get that wild on the men." That's because I'm not quite done with the men yet.

I do wholeheartedly believe that Christian females hold the key to the beginning of Revelation, but I also believe there are two gates. Christian men held the first key, and for the most part, we have completely left the gate open.

Let's go back and use the same scriptures I have already used to prop up my belief.

For the coming of the Son of Man will be just like the days of Noah.

—Matt. 24:37

That the sons of God saw that the daughters of men were beautiful; and they took wives for themselves, whomever they chose.

—Gen. 6:2

The sons of God looked upon the daughters of man and saw that they were beautiful. To me, what that means is that Christian men were looking at secular women with their braided hair, their gold jewelry, and their provocative clothing and thought how beautiful they were because these

Christian men were giving in to the lust of the flesh instead of seeing the beauty of a woman kneeling before the throne of God.

After Christian men walked away from these devout women, a new flock of young ladies saw the state of affairs and said, "Why would I kneel to this God? He offers nothing but loneliness on earth." Remember God's curse for the woman in the Garden of Eden? The cry of my heart is for my husband, but the Christian men that I know look at the brainless supermodels with lust. They look at these executive businesswomen with desire, these women who spend two hours in the gym because they have no kids, and my man has lust in his eyes. As a Christian woman, I must change my code of ethics and look outwardly beautiful to attract my Christian man because that seems to be what he is desiring.

And so, gentlemen, because of our wandering eyes, our women kneel to the world. Christian men, look within your heart. Look within your soul. Do you genuinely want arm candy, or do you genuinely want a woman who holds God above you? We as Christian men and I as a Christian man have fallen prey to this in the past, but how can we look at our women and say they're not measuring up to God's design when we are desiring the women our Christian females are emulating?

I've seen Christian men have lunch at Hooters. Are you freaking kidding me? Do you or do you not think that screams out, with a standing ovation, what you find pleasing?

Men of God, throw away the secular women. If you are married to a secular woman, I'm not saying to throw away your wife. The Bible is very clear what you are to do in 1 Corinthians 7.

What I'm saying is that if you are not married yet and are

pursuing a secular woman, leave her alone. Be an example for your brothers. Be an example for your sons. Be the example for all humanity that we hold a woman who loves God higher than any flesh, pretty eyes, nice booty, large baby nutrition delivery systems, or flirtatious words.

I cannot tell you which gate you should close first. I cannot even tell you if the gates can be closed, but I can tell you that if we as Christians do not close the gates, the events of Revelation will happen sooner rather than later. The Bible is very clear that there will be a great falling away, and it is happening. We are witnessing it.

> *Now we request you, brethren, with regard to the coming of our Lord Jesus Christ and our gathering together to Him, that you not be quickly shaken from your composure or be disturbed either by a spirit or a message or a letter as if from us, to the effect that the day of the Lord has come. Let no one in any way deceive you, for it will not come unless the apostasy comes first, and the man of lawlessness is revealed, the son of destruction.*
>
> —2 Thess. 2:1–3

That word is captured as:

ESV: rebellion	KJV: falling away
NKJV: falling away	NLT: great rebellion
NIV: rebellion	NASB: apostasy

That is the feminine noun for defection from truth, for falling away, for forsaking, according to *Strong's Concordance* at Blueletterbible.org.

I beg of you if it is within our power to push that off for another day, try to do it. I do not imply that God will suspend his will for our obedience, but we are to live as perfect as we can, and if it is within our power to push it off for even another minute by clinging to God and giving more people time to come to the salvation of Christ, shouldn't we try? Shouldn't we do everything in our power to love our Christian women and show them that their value is not how big their body parts are? Their value is how they serve the Lord, gentlemen. I'm going to tell you right here and right now that the massive problems we are seeing in our Christian females are our fault.

As fathers on earth, as brothers on earth, as husbands on earth, if we do not fix it, God will. We are not just hurting ourselves. For the love of the church, sacrifice your desires, your dreams, your goals, your ambitions, and especially your lust, for the betterment of your church family. We are at fault, men, and it's time we take back our religion. It's time we take it back from TV commercials, from Disney Channel idiot dads, from heresy-preaching television pastors, from New Age doctrines that are polluting the body of Christ, and especially from secular women who tell our wives they are not pretty enough or smart enough and don't do enough mom things. Mighty men of God, I call you to action to manage your family well. Teach your daughters what their true value is. Teach your sons what a beautiful woman looks like. Recognize the beautiful, godly traits in your wife. Embrace those traits, encourage those traits, and lead your whole family under the obedience of God.

I failed. I pray with every stitch of my body that you will not.

The wolf is already in the house, man of God. I ask you, "What are you going to do about it?" Do not do what Adam did and blame the woman for being relational as she was designed to be. Do not blame God for the wolf being allowed to live. Do not act like Adam if you are blessed with a marriage.

If you are blessed with a helper, just like employee appreciation is a real thing, spousal appreciation is too. Tonight, and every night for the rest of your life, show your wife that you appreciate her, not because she deserves it but because that might just be the one memory that keeps her from falling to sin. I am not saying to accept her sinful ways nor am I saying to look past her sinful ways. That must be addressed, but do it with love. Your only thoughts should be on the things of God and the kingdom of God, including doing your absolute best to make sure your wife has everything she needs to help you.

Take it from me, brother. If a woman does not feel like she helps you, she will find someone she does feel that way about, and then she will take her desire for her husband and latch it onto another person. It could be another male, but most likely it will be another female, and she will build an idol of that person because she finds true gratification, true appreciation, and true recognition from that person for her help.

To put it in military terms, you've been given a helper, so use it or lose it. The darkness wants nothing more than to feast on your unprotected woman. And gentlemen, as I've already stated, the wolf is in the house. That is completely our fault.

I could sit here and list every little thing that both of my ex-wives did wrong, but in the end, it does not matter. We were told to treat our wives with love. We often forget that, but as Christ oversees the church, so the man oversees the marriage.

Well, let's back engineer this a little bit. How did the church treat Christ? They were always hungry. The apostles were always messing things up. How many times did Christ's frustration show itself with the apostles? The leaders turned the church into a merchant's house. One of Jesus's apostles even betrayed him to his death.

Guess what Christ still did after that. Guess what he still does.

He gave his life for that church. He didn't play tit for tat. He didn't cry and throw a tantrum about how unfairly he had been treated. He treated the church with love, not just what it would be while he was on earth but what it would be even after he was gone. Christ to the church is to be our example of husband to wife.

In my opinion, to take on the mantle of a husband is to take on the most responsibility any human on this earth has ever taken on, other than Christ himself. In my opinion, pastors weren't even called to a higher level of responsibility than the man who is called to marriage. That is why I warn all of you young men to not rush into marriage. Wait until you're strong. Wait until you put away all the childish things. Wait until you are so solid in your relationship with God that when you receive the additional burden and blessing of a family, you will not let the wolf in the house.

While you are waiting, discipline your mind, discipline your faith, discipline your body, discipline your budget, and discipline your heart.

Every line of scripture you read is a tiny little victory for your family.

Every push-up, sit-up, and mile run is a grain of salt added to you.

Every time you look at a woman without lust is another line of code that reprograms your mind to value only the things of God.

Build yourself up into a biblical tank, that if God were to

put it on the battlefield it would be a beautiful tool in the war against unseen forces.

All men, I beg you to learn from me. Learn what not to do. Learn from my mistakes, for when you blame the employee for the condition of the company and then turn around and blame the CEO for hiring the employee you were put in charge of, death will surely follow. For those who didn't catch the reference, this is literally what Adam did in the Garden of Eden.

Stand for your God, and hate this world.

ROLES OF THE CHURCH

Why is this important?

It's important because church leaders are crazy and confusing. You confuse me with your different titles and who does what and which person gets a named parking space and all that mess.

I don't care about the 12 tribes, the nation of Israel, or the layout of a Jewish synagogue. I want to know about Christ's church and how the New Testament tells us to organize it. I want to know each person's role and what their qualifications are. Can they be women? Do they have authority? I want to know . . . so here we go.

If the Bible tells you to do something, should you do it?

But do not be called Rabbi; for One is your Teacher, and you are all brothers.

—Matt. 23:8

Here is the definition of *rabbi*, according to BlueLetterBible. org (G4461):

1. My great one, my honorable sir

2. A title used by the Jews to address their teachers (and also honor them when not addressing them

All right, so nobody is to be called rabbi, teacher, great one, or honorable sir.

Do not call anyone on earth your father; for One is your Father, He who is in heaven.

—Matt. 23:9

And don't call anyone father, not even the male who donated sperm for your conception. I, Glen, refer to him as Dad. I have a Father, and he is above. There is a difference between a male guardian earthly parent and a father. Christ is trying to help you understand that the people who told you what to do all your life, the ones you revere and hold in high standing—you are to *stop* calling them Father. They are people. Show appreciation, love them, and care for them, but understand that they are just people—fathers, grandfathers, stepfathers—but *not Fathers.*

When I have to fill out a government document and there is a section for "father," of course I write my dad's name there. This is the secular world's ignorance. Try putting a line through the word *father* and writing the word *dad*, they usually don't mind.

I do have older brothers who are wiser in the ways of the Word than I am. I cling to them and suck the knowledge from their heads like a leech. I am a vampire for the knowledge of God. But I always treat these men like they are my brothers, *not* as a father and not with reverence.

If Paul walked into this room, I would call him *Paul*—not Dr. Paul, not Pastor Paul, not Elder Paul, not Master Paul, not Father Paul. Paul. Paul. Paul.

Church leaders, *stop* giving yourselves titles. You will be judged for it. You will be judged harshly for making or allowing others to call you by your position. This is a reverence reserved for God, not you. You are *just a brother or sister*. Get over yourself. You are a servant just like me.

I cannot tell you how many times I have gone to a church and they say, "Here is Pastor Bob." It should be, "Here is one of the pastors of our church, Bob."

It is a job. It is your obedience to Christ. It is your *job*, not your *title*

If you want to play that game, church leaders, walk with me for a bit and let's play.

You do agree that all have fallen short of the glory of God, right?

And all Christians are equal to you, right?

From now on, why don't you refer to every Christian in your congregation by their title too?

School Teacher Debbie.

Police Officer Jones.

Cashier Robert.

United States Marine Ricky.

C'mon, Pastor Bobs of America, Father Mikes, *Reverend Jimmy*. *All* of you are in the sin of ignorance or the sin of pride. Stop it!

Your name is *Mike*. Your job is pastor. Stop letting it go to your head. There is another creature who got bruised on his head when he thought too much of himself (can't remember where I heard that).

You are a brother, so be a brother. Love our congregation. Respect our congregation. Oversee our congregation, *not* from above but right beside us. My Jesus is my High Priest, *not you*.

If my words stun you, *good*. We need to be "woke" the right way—the God way.

Church, if you wonder why our country has gone crazy, why people are leaving the church in droves, why Christian marriages don't last, why premarital sex is rampant, and why church leaders are as corrupt as everyone else, *look at our "leaders."*

Look at our shepherds who give themselves titles, wear fancy suits, drive a fancy car, live off the fat of the congregation, promote prosperity instead of God's Word, and promote mission trips to Costa Rica when there is a widow in the church who is losing her house. They are puffed up *chewers,* chewing on the Word of God like cattle instead of consuming it with their hearts and souls.

Do you think I am being mean? A little too harsh? Let's see what Christ said.

*Then Jesus spoke to the crowds and His disciples, saying: "The scribes and the Pharisees have seated themselves in the chair of Moses; therefore all that they tell you, do and observe, but do not do according to their deeds; for they say **things and do not do** them. They tie up heavy burdens and lay them on men's shoulders, but they themselves are unwilling to move them with so much as a finger. But they do all their deeds to be noticed by men; for they broaden their phylacteries and lengthen the tassels of their garments. They love the place of honor at banquets and the chief seats in the synagogues, and respectful greetings in the market places, and being called Rabbi by men. But do not be called Rabbi; for One is your Teacher, and you are all brothers. Do not call anyone on earth your father; for One is your Father, He who is in heaven. Do not be called leaders; for One is your Leader, that is, Christ. But the greatest among you shall be your* *servant. Whoever exalts himself shall be humbled; and whoever humbles himself shall be exalted.*

—Matt. 23:1–12

Whoever humbles himself shall be exalted. Are you humble cud-chewers? Does your life scream out humble? Or does it scream out luxury with that fancy car and that fancy house?

Whoa! Glen, you are taking this too far. We give them these titles as a sign of respect.

Uh-huh. Then they will give you all that same respect in return because, after all, as Christ said, we are all brothers and sisters. Live by the sword, die by the sword. Get titles, give titles. Check . . . and . . . mate.

No more titles, church. This is critical. I know it seems like I am making a mountain out of a molehill, but he who has ears, let him hear. There is judgment coming. It's better to be verbally smacked around by Glen and get it right than to be judged for misleading the church.

I have shed blood in the mud of the oilfields. I have worn the American flag on my Marine Corps uniform. I have had the state seal of law enforcement. I have also served time behind bars (one month when I was 17 years old) for a crime *I did* commit. I share genetics with three other men, all from the same mom. The point of all this is that I have a lot of brothers. I *know* what brotherhood is. None of us have titles when it comes down to it. We complied with the rules of the organization that brought us together. This organization, the true church under Christ, has told you not to use titles. You are all equal; you are all brothers and sisters.

Let me ask you this: do you have a sibling? Would you call them Dr. (insert their name) if they got a doctorate degree? Yeah, me neither. They are my brother, and I will treat them as such, even if they are more knowledgeable or wiser than I am.

Stop revering people. Stop lifting up any person on this planet above another. *Stop!*

Now for the church clergy who *are* humble, are pursuing the Word, and are loving. I love you dearly like a brother.

To the pastors who break bread with the congregation not just during ceremonies, I adore you. I have seen pastors slosh in the mud and the muck to fix a widow's fence. I've seen them covered from head to toe in dirt while working on the church property. To you people, may the Almighty bless you with every ounce I can beg.

To the bishops and deacons who give their personal phone numbers to their congregation, you are the backbone of our church. Stand firm, my family. Stand firm.

Elders, please keep watch for us. Please help us. We wander off, and the wolf is always near. Please stay strong for us.

I know being a shepherd is a laborious job that often leaves you emotionally and mentally drained, but we are worth it. We all serve a purpose. Together we can stand as one Christ-led church.

To the ministry workers whose fingers bleed, eyes burn, backs ache, and hearts pour out, I cannot express how much you mean to me. I just can't. The sympathy of the congregation when a person is in need is overwhelming. May God please bless you. Please.

All right, so let's see an actual role in the church.

An overseer, then, must be above reproach, the husband of one wife, temperate, prudent, respectable, hospitable, able to teach, not addicted to wine or pugnacious, but gentle, peaceable, free from the love of money. He must be one who manages his own household well, keeping his children under control with all dignity (but if a man does not know how to manage his own household, how will he take care of the church of God?), and not a new convert, so that he will not become conceited and fall into the condemnation incurred by the devil. And he must have a good reputation with those outside the church, so that he will not fall into reproach and the snare of the devil.

—1 Tim. 3:2–7

For this reason I left you in Crete, that you would set in order what remains and appoint elders in every city as I directed you, namely, if any man is beyond reproach, the husband of one wife, having children who believe, not accused of indecent behavior or rebellion. For the overseer must be beyond reproach as God's steward, not self-willed, not quick-tempered, not overindulging in wine, not a bully, not greedy for money, but hospitable, loving what is good, self-controlled, righteous, holy, disciplined, holding firmly the faithful word which is in accordance with the teaching, so that he will be able both to exhort in sound doctrine and to refute those who contradict it.

For there are many rebellious men, empty talkers and deceivers, especially those of the circumcision, who must be silenced because they are upsetting whole families, teaching things they should not teach for the sake of sordid gain. One of themselves, a prophet of their own, said, "Cretans are always liars, evil beasts, lazy gluttons." This testimony is true. For this reason reprove them severely so that they may be sound in the faith, not paying attention to Jewish myths and commandments of men who turn away from the truth. To the pure, all things are pure; but to those who are defiled and unbelieving, nothing is pure, but both their mind and their conscience are defiled. They profess to know God, but by their deeds they deny Him, being detestable and disobedient and worthless for any good deed.

—Titus 1:5–16

All right, so we have an elder of the church. He must be male, married, and have Christian kids. Either the Bible is your instruction manual . . . or it is not.

If you have a problem with this, you probably have a problem with Genesis where Eve was told that her desire will only be for her husband. I will discuss the perfect harmony of men and women later, but if elders can only be male bothers you, then you need to either pray for wisdom and take your problem to the church *or* accept that you have turned to the "commandments of men who turn away from the truth."

You're either in, or you are out.

I have seen an elder whose kid was running wild. Should that person have remained an elder? *No.* It may not be their fault, but that matters not. The qualifications do not change because someone "did their best." What if that person doesn't have a kid? Again, look at the qualifications.

If an elder's wife dies, that is horrible, and I mourn the loss, but it is time to step down, Mr. Elder. You either fit the bill, or you do not.

Deacons likewise must be men of dignity, not double-tongued, or addicted to much wine or fond of sordid gain, but holding to the mystery of the faith with a clear *conscience. These men must also first be tested; then let them serve as deacons if they are beyond reproach. Women must likewise be dignified, not malicious gossips, but temperate, faithful in all things. Deacons must be husbands of only **one wife**, and good managers of their children and their households. For those who have served well as deacons obtain for themselves a high standing and great confidence in the faith that is in Christ Jesus.*

—1 Tim. 3:8–13

What? A woman . . . deacon . . . huh?

I commend to you our sister Phoebe, who is a servant of the church which is at Cenchrea; that you receive her in the Lord in a manner worthy of the saints, and that you help her in whatever matter she may have need of you; for she herself has also been a helper of many, and of myself as well

—Rom. 16:1–2

Now, boys and girls, we can argue over this point . . . or we can just use some logic.

Paul—*the* Paul—says something like this: "Here is Phoebe. Do what she says."

Not enough? Okay.

Why would the deacon role require a deacon's wife's checklist but not an elder's wife's checklist? Sounds backward, doesn't it? An elder is higher than a deacon, right? So unless you're saying they are the same role, which they aren't because of the word *likewise*, clearly there is a difference here.

So what is the difference between the elder and the deacon? The difference is the requirements. Look at the requirements. Think of them as the hiring page of a job listing. "Must possess these skills . . . " Are these all the requirements? No, but it is the basics.

dignity	not insincere	Not prone to drink much wine	Not greedy for money
holding to the mystery of the faith with a clear conscience	beyond reproach	women, not malicious gossips	temperate, faithful in all things
husband of one wife	good managers of their children	good managers of their household	

Elders have to be ready for battle—biblical battle.

Holding fast the faithful word which is in accordance with the teaching, so that he will be able both to exhort in sound doctrine and to refute those who contradict.

—Titus 1:9

And they have to be hospitable.

True, it could be seen as a lesser position, but then Paul had to say this:

For those who have served well as deacons obtain for themselves a high standing and great confidence in the faith that is in Christ Jesus.

—1 Tim. 3:13

All right, church. We have elders ready to do battle. We have deacons moving things around.

Paul and Timothy, bond-servants of Christ Jesus,

To all the saints in Christ Jesus who are in Philippi, including the overseers and deacons.

—Phil. 1:1

Again, overseer just means elder.

Acts 20:17 – elders
Titus 1:5 – elders
1 Peter 5:1–14 – elders

But then we have something strange. The New American Standard Bible (NASB) does this:

He who descended is Himself also He who ascended far above all the heavens, so that He might fill all things. And He gave some as apostles, and some as prophets, and some as evangelists, and some as pastors and teachers, for the equipping of the saints for the work of service, to the building up of the body of Christ.

—Eph. 4:10–12

Pastors . . what? We had elders and deacons. The word *pastors* occur one time in the NASB, and that is right here. Let's go to my beloved King James Version (KJV). Yep, it's the same thing—*pastors.*

We have rules for elders and deacons but not for pastors, apostles, prophets, evangelists, and teachers?

Okay, let's do this another way. Let's define the above roles and see if that helps.

The table below is from BlueLetterBible.org referencing *Strong's Concordance.*

Term	Strong's Concordance	Definition
apostle	G652	A delegate, messenger, one sent forth with orders
prophet	G4396	One who, moved by the Spirit of God and hence his organ or spokesman, solemnly declares to men what he has received by inspiration, especially concerning future events, and in particular such, as relate to the cause and kingdom of God and human salvation
evangelist	G2099	A bringer of good tidings, an evangelist, the name given to the NT heralds of salvation through Christ who are not apostles
pastor	G4166	A herdsman, especially a shepherd
teacher	G1320	A teacher

Well, this is a strange list. We go from elder and deacon to a completely different list.

Here is the trick, my family. We need to rightly divide the Word. I am not a big Peter fan, but this man does crack the mystery wide open.

Therefore, I exhort the elders among you, as your fellow elder and witness of the sufferings of Christ, and a partaker also of the glory that is to be revealed,

—1 Pet. 5:1

Peter was an apostle *and* an elder.
Whoa!

From Miletus he sent to Ephesus and called to him the elders of the church.

—Acts 20:17

Be on guard for yourselves and for all the flock, among which the Holy Spirit has made you overseers, to shepherd the church of God which He purchased with His own blood.

—Acts 20:28

A pastor is a shepherd, and so is an elder. That is strange, I know, but just hang on. It gets a little weirder. Then I will turn on the lights for those who can't see.

But where does the deacon fit in?

We need to break this word down. The definition according to *Strong's Concordance* (G1249) at BlueLetterBible.org is "one who executes the commands of another especially of a master, a servant, attendant, or minister."

What? Deacon = attendant, servant, or minister?

Here we go, family. Enough confusion.

There are two schools of thought.

The first is a church body.

For this situation, elders are appointed. Everyone who is an elder is a pastor. The term is interchangeable.

Deacons work under them.

Teachers can be an elder *or* deacon, but they can also be someone the elders of the church have vetted fully. These are the people who go from church to church teaching or just randomly show up once in a while to give a sermon. The role is 100 percent at the mercy of the elders since it is the elders' job to protect the flock. The teacher is teaching the flock.

Evangelists should be an elder since they have to do biblical battle at some point, but I could see a situation where they could also be a deacon.

Prophets don't work for anyone on Earth. They are outside of church regulation. They are the wild card. I will break this down in a bit.

Apostle is a retired term. It was retired when the last apostle died. Apostles initially brought the news of Christ to the Jews. Later, Paul, the Gentiles' apostle, brought the news to us. They were all *directly* given the commission by Jesus Christ himself. Those given the commission to bring the good news of Christ forward are now evangelists.

Here it is as a table for my visual family members.

Apostles	Retired
Prophets	Wild card
Evangelists	Elder (should be)
Pastors	Elder
Teachers	Under elder oversight

But Glen, I am a worship leader at a church. Really? Didn't Christ tell you not to call yourself a leader?

Do not be called leaders; for One is your Leader, that is, Christ.

—Matt. 23:10

Well, gosh-geez, Glen. I can't call Pastor Bob my church leader? No! He is not a leader; he is supposed to be an obeyer. We are all brothers and sisters—*all* of us. No one is higher than another. We all fall short of the glory of God.

Mr. or Mrs. Worship Leader, your biblical title is worship deacon, or maybe worship elder, but you need to be ready to do biblical battle if you take on that title.

"I am the Children's Ministry Director." No, you are either an elder or a deacon.

"I am the Executive Pastor." Okay, the term is interchangeable—Executive Elder or Executive Pastor—it doesn't change a thing. Rock on, EP, rock on.

Family, I have been to a lot of churches, and every one of them is different—every single church. And that is against the Bible. He says they are wrong; they say we are wrong. How about this? How about that?

Enough Chaos!

How about instead of finding out who is wrong, we just cling to what is right?

The Bible has given you *very* specific job titles to use in the church. *Stop making up new titles!* Stop! Stop! Stop!

You are making up titles and confusing the congregation about who must comply with what rules. Stop!

Below are some titles in the church that need to be eliminated *right now*.

Pope	Priest	Chaplain
Monk/Friar	Father	Monsignor
Legate	Majordomo	Nuncio
Delegate	Moderator	Missionary
Pastor's First Lady	Cardinal	Nun
Ministry Leader	Worship Leader	Director
Reverend	Doctor	Preacher

Ministering just means caring for. If all of us are following the will of God, the example of Jesus, the direction of the Holy Spirit, and the instruction of the Bible, then *we are all ministers*.

The church is shepherded not by a single pastor but by a group of pastors. Do you understand me, church? A group. The terms *pastor* and *elder* are interchangeable. The King James Version calls them bishops. And that is okay, too, because it gives us the qualifications of the bishop, who is an elder/pastor.

But never is there to be a single pastor. If one of the pastors is titled pastor, then they *all* are. Pastor doesn't mean the guy talking behind the pulpit. Pastor is the entire group of people shepherding that church. All are pastors or elders or bishops.

Church leadership must be above reproach. When we just make up titles, it gets blurry what their qualifications should be according to God. Is the Bible God's Word? Shouldn't we listen to it?

Churches will have paid staff and volunteer positions

that, because of hiring requirements, basic logic, and ease of coordination need to have a title. The big difference I am talking about is the people in positions of responsibility—real responsibility. I am not talking about Chuck the paid crossing guard. I am talking about your Children's Director who is literally in charge of curriculum for all the Sunday school kids of a big church. Shouldn't this person have some real rules put on them? Shouldn't they be God-sized rules and not just the traditions of man? This is Christ's church, right? Didn't the apostles tell us how to set the church up? What "in the name of God" are you doing?

You were told how to do it, and this is what you decided to do, church elders? Don't make me stop this car.

Moving on . . .

Do you remember that wild card I told you about, that other school of thought?

Congregation, there is a back door that Christ/God/Holy Spirit built into the church body to ensure that people near and far, high and low, and all over the earth could always get to their King regardless of misled "leaders."

Therefore, since we have a great high priest who has passed through the heavens, Jesus the Son of God, let us hold fast our confession.

—Heb. 4:14

Christ is our High Priest. He is in charge of the church.

But the Helper, the Holy Spirit, whom the Father will send in My name, He will teach you all things, and bring to your remembrance all that I said to you.

—John 14:26

91

The Holy Spirit that Christ sent will be your teacher. If you don't believe me, let me explain further.

*I have many more things to say to you, but you cannot bear them now. But when He, the Spirit of truth, comes, He will guide you into all the truth; for He will not speak on His own initiative, but whatever He hears, He will speak; and He will disclose to you what is to come. He will glorify Me, for He will take of Mine and will disclose it to you. All things that the Father has are Mine; therefore I said that He takes of Mine and will disclose it **to you.***

—John 16:12–15

But you are a chosen race, a royal priesthood, a holy nation, a people for God's own possession, so that you may proclaim the excellencies of Him who has called you out of darkness into His marvelous light; for you once were not a people, but now you are the people of God; you had not received mercy, but now you have received mercy.

—1 Pet. 2:9–10

Pastors and deacons are guides, people who have hopefully heard the call from on high to help guide us like shepherds to greener pastures. They are guides.

We are all sheep, right?

Most of us imagine a sheep as a soft, little, fluffy, cute, baby lamb. I want you to pull out your cell phone and type this into your favorite search engine: South Dakota Bighorn

Ram/Sheep. That thing is crazy strong. It can weigh up to 315 pounds, live all over the place, navigate mountains climbing up almost sheer walls, and fight over women. Check out "Big Horn Sheep Battle" on YouTube. Now that is a sheep. This is what our flock was supposed to be—sturdy in the Lord, rugged.

If our overseers aren't fit, don't worry. We have Jesus, we have the Holy Spirit, and we have God's prophets.

What, Glen? You can't just slide the prophets in there!

Oh, yes I can. The prophets were wild.

Ezekiel laid down for 390 days straight. Hosea named his kids "Not Loved" and "Not My People." Isaiah walked around naked—for three years.

The prophets were told to deliver a wide range of messages to the people. Isaiah told Judah to be faithful to God 150 years before their exile. Daniel told Israel they would be saved.

God has sent prophets to the congregations to warn them in provocative ways.

The Lord said to me, 'They have spoken well. I will raise up a prophet from among their countrymen like you, and I will put My words in his mouth, and he shall speak to them all that I command him. It shall come about that whoever will not listen to My words which he shall speak in My name, I Myself will require it of him.

—Deut. 18:17–19

When the church gets too crazy, God always drops people on us to fix us or at least warn us. In the Old Testament, God had his prophets. In the days of Christ, Jesus had his apostles.

Blueletterbible.org

Prophets	G4396	One who, moved by the Spirit of God and hence his organ or spokesman, solemnly declares to men what he has received by inspiration, especially concerning future events, and in particular such, as relate to the cause and kingdom of God and to human salvation

The Holy Spirit, who is now within us, either has or will have his prophets. I think of it like a person on a specific mission—a very, very specific mission—for God.

In my opinion, these are the people tasked with something daunting—a task comparable to being beheaded, being stoned (not with drugs), walking around naked, and all the other things God's previous prophets and Jesus's apostles endured. We are in the age of the Holy Spirit on earth. The Book of Acts recorded this event, the fulfillment of the Lord's Feast of Pentecost. We can debate modern-day prophets at a later time, but for now, for this chapter, please walk away from the world's tactics of making up titles for people so they don't have to comply with the prerequisites outlined in the Bible.

We need to remember our first love. We need to *stop* revolting against the Bible. We need to stop diluting our biblical lemonade. I can hardly taste the lemon anymore. Stop! Stop now. It will only lead to your ruin.

No more titles. Stop holding men and women in reverence. God warned you that he is a jealous God. You have been warned. It is God and you with nothing in between.

I will end this chapter with two things we should all remember.

Let not many of you become teachers, my brethren, knowing that as such we will incur a stricter judgment.

—James 3:1

If you do have a good biblical teacher, one who cares about making sure you understand to the best of your specific capabilities, one who is always there, one who is free with the knowledge, please show them appreciation. When the class is over, don't jump up and run out the door. Let them know how much you appreciate them, their hard work, and their patience. Teaching the Bible is exhausting if you are reading the room right. These men and women deserve *not praise*, but certainly some genuine sibling affection. Buy them a coffee. Bring in an extra pack of pens. Put the chairs up, and help clean the room. Do something, anything. Love them.

Whatever you do in word or deed, do all in the name of the Lord Jesus, giving thanks through Him to God the Father.

—Col. 3:17

If your church is in the wrong, bring this information to your elders. Ask them to explain why we are deviating from the Bible. If their answers don't line up with the Bible, it might be time to start church shopping or even correct this elder.

It is time to come out of the darkness, church. Rome is burning. Find your faith. Read your Bible, not for me, not because Bob the pastor told you to, but for you. If you get stumped, call your elder, call a deacon, phone your small group, or phone a friend. In the worst case, pick up your social media device (aka cell phone), type in the verse address, and type "explain" at the end of it.

Information has greatly multiplied, including Bible information. Use it or lose it. Grow in your faith and knowledge, or be destroyed. We are in the process of sanctification, and I pray that you will not give up on yourself. Find strength. Pray for strength to endure. Pray for wisdom. Pray for knowledge.

One church, one goal, one set of titles for the church, regardless of the city, state, or country. If we are one body, shouldn't we have the same "DNA"?

I know a lot of people are going to read this book, even this chapter, and say I am crossing hairs here. I am taking a small issue and making it a big one, they might say.

Go listen to Casting Crowns' song "Slow Fade." Go. Right now.

All done? Good.

We give up the holidays in the Bible, the Lord's feasts. We accept new ones like Christmas (not in the Bible) and Easter (not in the Bible). We ignore the baptism of fire and embrace the baptism of water. We give up our proper church titles and make up new ones so they can have the responsibility without the checklist.

We address people by their titles with reverence. We work on the Sabbath. We work during the Lord's feasts. We took the husband-wife marriage and made it open to any gender.

We accept that the person in the pulpit is good because they are standing on the stage instead of testing their spirit like we have been told to do.

We are fading.

The current state of our church is a "slow fade." We are losing our saltiness, and we need to stop the erosion.

Cling to that which is good. These man-made things that go against what the Bible instructs must stop. As a church, we violate the Bible all the time, and most of us don't even know it.

Do you want another example?

Again, you have heard that the ancients were told, "You shall not make false vows, but shall fulfill your vows to the Lord." But I say to you, make no oath at all, either by heaven, for it is the throne of God, or by the earth, for it is the footstool of His feet, or by Jerusalem, for it is the city of the great King. Nor shall you make an oath by your head, for you cannot make one hair white or black. But let your statement be, "Yes, yes" or "No, no"; anything beyond these is of evil.

—Matt. 5:33–37

Does anyone know of any ceremony that requires you to "swear in"?

"Please raise your right hand and swear . . . "

Yes, folks, we go against the Bible all the time. It is time we take our religion back—true Christians, true Christianity, faithfulness to the Bible, faithfulness to our Christ. These are his words. Do you follow him or not?

I, Glen Penn, swore into the United States Marine Corps. I "swore in" a few more times throughout my 20s. I violated that too. But we can't keep going against Christ, not as a church and not as an individual.

I love you, but it is time to stand up.

97

MEDITATION

Why is this important?

There are a million verses that tell us to think about things.

> *Do not neglect the spiritual gift within you, which was bestowed on you through prophetic utterance with the laying on of hands by the presbytery. Take pains with these things; be **absorbed in them**, so that your progress will be evident to all. Pay close attention to yourself and your teaching; persevere in these things, for as you do this you will ensure salvation both for yourself and for those who hear you.*
>
> —1 Tim. 4:14–16

The above is Paul talking specifically to Timothy, but he has sound direction. There is a large list of things Paul told him to be absorbed in, including being an example of discipline, love, faith, and purity.

Biblical meditation, to my understanding, isn't getting into a specific position, chanting, and opening imaginary eyes. Biblical meditation is also known as reflection time, time to dwell, time to pray, and time to be still in the Lord.

Here is what I have done in the past in case it might help you.

I get in the bathtub and crank up the water. When it is full, I turn it off and lay back. Slowly I lower my head into the water until only my mouth, nose, and closed eyes are sticking up. I am 6 feet tall, so my legs stick up as I go down. It is what it is.

With the world completely calm and my ears submerged, I mentally form an image. I see a woodland area—not cold or creepy woods but warm woods with light randomly breaking through the trees. I am standing on pine needles with the springtime breeze gently blowing. Random grass and small bushes are scattered around, but the area I am in is pretty clear. I look through the tree line, and nearby is an open field. Deer walk by, and the birds are softly making bird noises. The world is serene.

Anytime anything mentally bubbles up, I go back to this woodland image. This is my neutral state throughout this exercise.

As I am standing there, I see a comfy-looking tree stump that I go sit on. I sit down and get situated. Gently, a warm, glowing ball appears in front of me and slowly materializes into what I imagine Christ to be. My mind sees him as a Middle Eastern man—skinny, long hair, beard, friendly smile, slow deliberate speech, and warm eyes.

He looks at me, and our eyes meet like my most trusted person has been waiting for me and I have finally arrived.

We stare for a bit. I'm just drinking in his presence, and he's giving me time. He gives me a nod; I nod back, and we begin.

Gently he asks, "Why are you troubled"?

I tell him my biggest worry. The last time was my relationship with my wife.

"Whom do you serve?"

I tell him, "You."

"Am I a good Shepherd?"

I say yes.

"Why do you not trust me?"

I tell him because I try to do the work myself. I think I should be better, and I think that he and the world deserve me to be better. I make too many mistakes.

He smiles gently and asks, "Who is in charge of it all?"

I tell him God.

He asks, "Who is in complete control of it all?"

I tell him God.

"Are you trying as best you can?"

I tell him yes, but my best isn't . . .

He gently cuts me off. "Yes or no?"

I tell him yes.

"Am I fair and understanding?"

I tell him yes.

"Do you think I require more than your absolute best effort?"

I tell him no.

"Then why are you still troubled?"

I tell him because I haven't done enough.

He smirks a little and asks, "Did I do enough?"

I smile back and say yes.

He asks, "Why are you hiding from me?"

I explain because it isn't going right, and I bear fault in that. I am messing things up, even if only in part.

His smile broadens as he says, "Whom do you serve?"

I tell him, "You."

He asks, "Why do you think it is messed up?"

Because I say, it is not how I think it should be.

His smile is huge now, his eyes wide open as he asks, "Who is in charge?"

I kick a rock in my mind and stick out my childish, fat lip and say, "Not me."

We sit there on those stumps, talking back and forth. I pour out my failings, and he just asks question after question about everything from my worries about the future to my children, to make amends, to sibling fights, to work, to bills. Everything gets trivialized under "his control" and "did I do my best." Sometimes I tell him I did not, and he asks back, "What should you do about it?"

This is one of the practices that I hold dear, learning time and again to let God handle godly matters. I was told to put on the light yoke that Christ offers, yet time and again I pull against the reins trying to get it done faster or better or harder. Every time he asks, "Who is in charge?"

My favorite one is when I complain about stupid stuff, and he asks, "Are you in prison?" "Are you starving?" "How many shirts do you have in your closet?"

We go back and forth until I realize I am blessed and doing exactly what my sinful nature compels me to do, which is looking for the negative.

This is one of my mental strategies to slow down. I do *not* believe I am actually talking to Christ. It is more likely the Holy Spirit, but I wouldn't try to make that claim either. Between you and me, I also wouldn't be too surprised if I get up there and find out it was the Holy Spirit. That would be cool—like really, really cool.

My family, this is how I dwell on my troubles and failures. This is how I go through some of the harshest things in life, hold onto joy, and smile through it. This is how I made it through childhood abuse, horrible relationships, war zones, prison riots, drugs and more drugs, divorce, church problems, and standing up in the mission I was given.

That requires practice. It requires a calm place. It requires cutting out some time to just dwell. Church, if you are not taking time to just dwell on the Spirit, dwell on Christ, dwell on your understandings, and dwell on your emotional thoughts, you are doing yourself a great disservice.

Talk to the Holy Spirit. He will teach you. Calm your mind, and talk.

If a thought bubbles through—"Did I put a peanut butter sandwich in little Sally's lunch today?"—stop the conversation, and go back to your version of the tree stump. See the deer. Make yourself see the deer. Then hear the birds. Then see the light.

Control your mind.

I am ADHD. If I can do this after years of practice, so can you. Discipline your mind.

Read your Bible.

Talk to Jesus. Talk to God. Talk to the Holy Spirit.

Talk to the elders of your church. They should know you by your first name. They should know your problems so they can help shepherd you to greener pastures.

Find your peace church. If your church is full of gossips, chewers, troubled elders, bad memories, or whatever, go somewhere else. Find a place that lifts you up biblically. Find a place that nurtures your soul with love, compassion, and knowledge. Search for the place that embraces you and lifts you higher so you can lift others higher. Find a place that wants to make a disciple of you so you can make disciples of others one day.

Ain't none of us getting out of this alive, so we had better make the absolute best of it while we can.

My best life is *not* now. It is in heaven, but here on earth, I can find joy even when I am going through tribulation.

I can find peace when everyone is at war.

I can find freedom when everyone is chained down.

I can find strength when all hope looks lost.

I can find healing when everything is broken.

I can find God when darkness surrounds me.

God is in control. Take a moment to breathe that into your lungs.

ANGELS

Many of the people in the congregation are very misled about who, what, and why angels exist. First, if you are not a Christian, I am not talking to you. I love you, and we can share an ice-cold drink, but this is for Bible-believing Christians. If non-Christians want to believe whatever they want about angels, they are more than welcome to. I have not been called to correct the non-believer.

But if you do call yourself a Christian, if you say the Bible is your godly reference for what the Lord has done and how you should live, I am talking directly to you.

Here are some common ideas:

Angels are sitting on our shoulders and looking out for us. Each of us has a personal guardian angel who keeps us out of trouble.

Angels are amazing beings who want us to be happy.

Angels have wings and halos and play musical instruments. They're kind of like God's backup singers, and they look like babies.

Angels are better than humans in some way.

People become angels when they die.

Angels know everything.

We are going to dive pretty deeply into this because this needs to be cleared up.

First, let's look at angels' classifications. There are four classifications of angels referenced in the Bible—only four. Anything else you hear about does not come from the Protestant Bible.

Cherubim
Seraphim
Archangel
Angel

Each group looks a bit different, so let's take a closer look.

Gen. 16:7	Gen. 16:9	Gen. 16:10	Gen. 16:11	Gen. 21:17
Gen. 22:11	Gen. 22:15	Gen. 24:7	Gen. 24:40	Gen. 31:11
Gen. 48:16	Exod. 3:2	Exod. 14:19	Exod. 23:20	Exod. 23:23
Exod. 32:34	Exod. 33:2	Num. 20:16	Num. 22:22	Num. 22:23
Num. 22:24	Num. 22:25	Num. 22:26	Num. 22:27	Num. 22:31
Num. 22:32	Num. 22:34	Num. 22:35	Judg. 2:1	Judg. 2:4
Judg. 5:23	Judg. 6:11	Judg. 6:12	Judg. 6:20	Judg. 6:22
Judg. 13:3	Judg. 13:6	Judg. 13:9	Judg. 13:13	Judg. 13:15
Judg. 13:16	Judg. 13:17	Judg. 13:18	Judg. 13:19	Judg. 13:20
Judg. 13:21	1 Sam. 29:9	2 Sam. 14:17	2 Sam. 14:20	2 Sam. 19:27
2 Sam 24:16	2 Sam. 24:17	1 Kings 13:18	1 Kings 19:5	1 Kings 19:7
2 Kings 1:3	2 Kings 19:35	1 Chron. 21:15	1 Chron. 21:16	1 Chron. 21:18
1 Chron. 21:20	1 Chron. 21:27	1 Chron. 21:30	2 Chron. 32:21	Ps. 35:5
Ps. 35:6	Eccles. 5:6	Isa. 37:36	Isa. 63:9	Dan. 3:28
Dan. 6:22	Hos. 12:4	Zech. 1:9	Zech. 1:11	Zech. 1:12
Zech. 1:13	Zech. 1:14	Zech. 1:19	Zech. 2:3	Zech. 3:1
Zech. 3:3	Zech. 3:5	Zech. 3:6	Zech. 4:1	Zech. 4:4

Zech. 4:5	Zech. 5:5	Zech. 5:10	Zech. 6:4	Zech 6:5
Zech. 12:8	Matt. 1:20	Matt. 1:24	Matt. 2:13	Matt. 2:19
Matt. 28:2	Matt. 28:5	Luke 1:11	Luke 1:13	Luke 1:18
Luke 1:19	Luke 1:26	Luke 1:28	Luke 1:30	Luke 1:34
Luke 1:35	Luke 1:38	Luke 2:9	Luke 2:10	Luke 2:13
Luke 2:21	Luke 22:43	John 5:4	John 12:29	Acts 5:19
Acts 6:15	Acts 7:30	Acts 7:35	Acts 7:38	Acts 8:26
Acts 10:3	Acts 10:7	Acts 10:22	Acts 11:13	Acts 12:7
Acts 12:8	Acts 12:9	Acts 12:10	Acts 12:11	Acts 12:15
Acts 12:23	Acts 23:8	Acts 23:9	Acts 27:23	2 Cor. 11:14
Gal. 1:8	Gal. 4:14	Rev. 1:1	Rev. 2:1	Rev. 2:8
Rev. 2:12	Rev. 2:18	Rev. 3:1	Rev. 3:7	Rev. 3:14
Rev. 5:2	Rev. 7:2	Rev. 8:3	Rev. 8:7	Rev. 8:8
Rev. 8:10	Rev. 8:12	Rev. 8:13	Rev. 9:1	Rev. 9:11
Rev. 9:13	Rev. 9:14	Rev. 10:1	Rev. 10:5	Rev. 10:7
Rev. 10:8	Rev. 10:9	Rev. 11:1	Rev. 11:15	Rev. 14:6
Rev. 14:8	Rev. 14:9	Rev. 14:15	Rev. 14:17	Rev. 14:18
Rev. 14:19	Rev. 16:3	Rev. 16:4	Rev. 16:5	Rev. 16:8
Rev. 16:10	Rev. 16:12	Rev. 16:17	Rev. 17:17	Rev. 18:1
Rev. 18:21	Rev. 19:17	Rev. 20:1	Rev. 21:17	Rev. 22:6
Rev. 22:8	Rev. 22:16			

Did you get all that?

No, Glen is not going to do that to you, but I did want to give you a reference page to be able to use as you see fit. I got the list from BlueLetterBible.org, referencing *Strong's Concordance*.

Those verses are every single time the specific term *angel* is used in the Bible. To be more accurate, it is the term *angelos*, and that term is accurately translated as "messenger."

With that cleared up, let's look at what these beings look like.

First, when Adam and Eve were kicked out of the Garden of Eden, God placed a cherubim and a flaming sword to guard it (Gen. 3:24). The next mention is when God laid out the dimensions of the Ark of the Covenant (Exod. 25) and the tabernacle curtains (Exod. 26).

In Exodus 37 we get a description of "their wings" being spread over the mercy seat, almost like a guard here too.

*The cherubim had their **wings** spread upward, covering the mercy seat with their wings, with their faces toward each other; the faces of the cherubim were toward the mercy seat.*

—Exod. 37:9

Ezekiel 10:7 says they have hands.

Then the cherub stretched out his hand from between the cherubim to the fire which was between the cherubim, took some and put it into the hands of the one clothed in linen, who took it and went out.

—Ezek. 10:7

In 2 Samuel 22:1–10, David is calling upon God—"Sheol surrounded me" and ungodly men made him afraid.

In 2 Samuel 22:11, God rides on a cherub.

And He rode on a cherub and flew;

And He appeared on the wings of the wind.

—2 Sam. 22:11

The reference to the Lord here is assumed to be the Son before he became man. So here is Christ riding on a cherub. Do you still think this is a baby with a harp?

Let's run the tally: wings, hands, able to be ridden.

And now we squirrel for a moment.

Within it, there were figures resembling four living beings. And this was their appearance: they had human form. Each of them had four faces and four wings. Their legs were straight and their feet were like a calf's hoof, and they gleamed like burnished bronze. Under their wings on their four sides were **human hands**. *As for the faces and wings of the four of them, their wings touched one another; their faces did not turn when they moved, each went straight forward. As for the form of their faces, each had the face of a man; all four had the face of a lion on the right and the face of a bull on the left, and all four had the face of an eagle. Such were their faces. Their wings were spread out above; each had two touching another being, and two covering their bodies. And each went straight forward; wherever the spirit was about to go, they would go, without turning as they went. In the midst of the living beings there was something that looked like burning coals of fire, like torches darting back and forth among the living beings. The fire was bright, and lightning was flashing from the fire. And the living beings ran to and fro like bolts of lightning.*

—Ezek. 1:5–14

This was the appearance of the four living creatures—four faces and four wings, straight feet like a calf, the color of brass, hands, and face of a man, the face of a lion, the face of an ox, the face of an eagle. Their appearance was like burning coals of fire, and out of the fire went forth lightning.

Keep in mind that this is Ezekiel's vision.

In Ezekiel 10 these hybrid things show back up.

And each one had four faces. The first face was the face of a cherub, the second face was the face of a man, the third the face of a lion, and the fourth the face of an eagle.

—Ezek. 10:14

So we have two different lists from the same author.

Ezekiel 1: man, lion, ox, eagle

Ezekiel 10: cherub, man, lion, eagle

What is the difference? The ox.

So a cherub has the face of an ox.

Let's run the tally again: wings, hands, able to be ridden, and an ox face.

Cherubim/ cherub	wings, hands, able to be ridden, an ox face	Guards/ mounts
Seraphim		
Archangel		
Angel		

If you ever wonder why there was so much bull worshiping in days past, it is because those people (or their ancestors) saw, actually saw, cherubim and began to worship those beings. That is why the Bible tells us over and over again *not* to worship angels because people—not God's people but heathen, pagan crazies—were doing that.

ENOUGH CHAOS

They made a calf in Horeb
And worshiped a molten image.
Thus they exchanged their glory
For the image of an ox that eats grass.
They forgot God their Savior,
Who had done great things in Egypt.

—Ps. 106:19–21

By the way, do we still hold to that little fluffy, winged baby idea? Yeah, it gets worse.

Up next we have the seraphim.

Isaiah 6 is the only place in the Bible they are referenced.

In the year of King Uzziah's death, I saw the Lord sitting on a throne, lofty and exalted, with the train of His robe filling the temple. Seraphim stood above Him, each having six wings: with two he covered his face, and with two he covered his feet, and with two he flew. And one called out to another and said,

"Holy, Holy, Holy, is the Lord of hosts, The whole earth is full of His glory."

And the foundations of the thresholds trembled at the voice of him who called out, while the temple was filling with smoke. Then I said,

"Woe is me, for I am ruined!
Because I am a man of unclean lips,
And I live among a people of unclean lips;
For my eyes have seen the King, the Lord of hosts."

Then one of the seraphim flew to me with a burning coal in his hand, which he had taken from the altar with tongs.

110

He touched my mouth with it and said, "Behold, this has touched your lips; and your iniquity is taken away and your sin is forgiven."

—Isa. 6:1–7

Church, something really strange happened here. This messenger first announced the Lord, and then Isaiah said, "I suck. I have unclean lips."

Next, one of the seraphim gets a coal and purges the sin off of Isaiah's lips. And *now* Isaiah can speak in the presence of the Lord, and he says one of my favorite verses in the entire Bible: "Here am I. Send me" (Isa. 6:8).

For the seraphim, I call this position "bailiff." He announced and made sure the area was ready for the Lord's business. There may be a better title for this position, but we only get these seven verses to form a mold. It's not a lot, but it's enough to get an idea. They are part herald, part constable, almost like the bailiff in a modern-day American courtroom. "All rise! The honorable Judge Bobby Bob . . . "

Cherubim	wings, hands, able to be ridden, and an ox face	Guards/mounts
Seraphim	6 wings, hands, talks . . . a lot Face and feet are *covered* by wings	Court bailiff
Archangel		
Angel		

As a catch-up, we have an Oxen-Pegasus mount and a tongue-burning fly-boy who is afraid of sunburns on his head and feet. I'm just poking a little fun, but to be honest, these were the least terrifying of the angels.

Next, we have the archangel. Below is *every single time* an archangel is referenced. There are a lot of people who make good, convincing arguments for other terms to be aliases of the term *archangel*, but let's keep to strict and obvious mentions for the moment.

> *Now it came about when Joshua was by Jericho, that he lifted up his eyes and looked, and behold, a man was standing opposite him with his sword drawn in his hand, and Joshua went to him and said to him, "Are you for us or for our adversaries?" He said, "No; rather I indeed come now as **captain of the host of the** Lord." And Joshua fell on his face to the earth, and bowed down, and said to him, "What has my lord to say to his servant?" The captain of the Lord's **host** said to Joshua, "Remove your sandals from your feet, for the place where you are standing is holy." And Joshua did so.*

—Josh. 5:13–15

Congregation, this was just weird. In Joshua 5, the Lord passed down to Israel that they needed to circumcise themselves. Then they ran out of the manna they were given, and then this happens.

Joshua 6 goes right back to non-angel events. Strange.

> *But the prince of the kingdom of Persia was withstanding me for twenty-one days; then behold, Michael, one of the chief princes, came to help me, for I had been left there with the kings of Persia.*

—Dan. 10:13

Then he said, "Do you understand why I came to you? But I shall now return to fight against the prince of Persia; so I am going forth, and behold, the prince of Greece is about to come. However, I will tell you what is inscribed in the writing of truth. Yet there is no one who stands firmly with me against these forces except Michael your prince.

—Dan. 10:20–21

Now at that time Michael, the great prince who stands guard **over the sons of your people**, will arise. And there will be a time of distress such as never occurred since there was a nation until that time; and at that time your people, everyone who is found written in the book, will be rescued. Many of those who sleep in the dust of the ground will awake, these to everlasting life, but the others to disgrace and everlasting contempt. Those who have insight will shine brightly like the brightness of the expanse of heaven, and those who lead the many to righteousness, like the stars forever and ever. But as for you, Daniel, conceal these words and seal up the book until the end of time; many will go back and forth, and knowledge will increase.

—Dan. 12:1–4

For the Lord Himself will descend from heaven with a shout, with the voice of the **archangel** and with the trumpet of God, and the dead in Christ will rise first.

—1 Thess. 4:16

Yet in the same way, these men, also by dreaming, defile the flesh, reject authority, and revile angelic majesties. But Michael the archangel, when he disputed with the devil and argued about the body of Moses, did not dare pronounce against him a railing judgment, but said, "The Lord rebuke you!" But these men revile the things which they do not understand; and the things which they know by instinct, like unreasoning animals, by these things they are destroyed.

—Jude 1:8–10

And there was war in heaven, Michael and his angels waging war with the dragon. The dragon and his angels waged war, and they were not strong enough, and there was no longer a place found for them in heaven. And the great dragon was thrown down, the serpent of old who is called the devil and Satan, who deceives the whole world; he was thrown down to the earth, and his angels were thrown down with him.

—Rev. 12:7–9

So that is an archangel.

He has a sword and wages war with Satan, the lord of hosts, the chief prince. It is alluded to that his voice is "extra." Other than this, I can see no difference between this archangel and other angels. Can you? Can you see a difference using the Bible?

There are a lot of people who try to also call the angel Gabriel an archangel. Here is a lot of scripture. You judge for yourself.

When I, Daniel, had seen the vision, I sought to understand it; and behold, standing before me was one who looked like a man. And I heard the voice of a man between the banks of Ulai, and he called out and said, "Gabriel, give this man an understanding of the vision." So he came near to where I was standing, and when he came I was frightened and fell on my face; but he said to me, "Son of man, understand that the vision pertains to the time of the end." Now while he was talking with me, I sank into a deep sleep with my face to the ground; but he touched me and made me stand upright. He said, "Behold, I am going to let you know what will occur at the final period of the indignation, for it pertains to the appointed time of the end.

—Dan. 8:15–19

While I was still speaking in prayer, then the man Gabriel, whom I had seen in the vision previously, came to me in my extreme weariness about the time of the evening offering. He gave me instruction and talked with me and said, "O Daniel, I have now come forth to give you insight with understanding. At the beginning of your supplications the command was issued, and I have come to tell you, for you are highly esteemed; so give heed to the message and gain understanding of the vision.

—Dan. 9:21–23

And an angel of the Lord appeared to him, standing to the right of the altar of incense. Zacharias was troubled when he saw the angel, and fear gripped him. But the angel said to him, "Do not be afraid, Zacharias, for your petition has been heard, and your wife Elizabeth will bear you a son, and you will give him the name John. You will have joy and gladness, and many will rejoice at his birth. For he will be great in the sight of the Lord; and he will drink no wine or liquor, and he will be filled with the Holy Spirit while yet in his mother's womb. And he will turn many of the sons of Israel back to the Lord their God. It is he who will go as a forerunner before Him in the spirit and power of Elijah, to turn the hearts of the fathers back to the children, and the disobedient to the attitude of the righteous, so as to make ready a people prepared for the Lord."

Zacharias said to the angel, "How will I know this for certain? For I am an old man and my wife is advanced in years." The angel answered and said to him, "I am Gabriel, who stands in the presence of God, and I have been sent to speak to you and to bring you this good news.

—Luke 1:11–19

Now in the sixth month the angel Gabriel was sent from God to a city in Galilee called Nazareth, to a virgin engaged to a man whose name was Joseph, of the descendants of David; and the virgin's name was Mary.

—Luke 1:26–27

This angel, Gabriel, was a messenger. In Daniel 10, Michael the archangel had to come to help Gabriel.

But the prince of the kingdom of Persia was withstanding me for twenty-one days; then behold, Michael, one of the

*chief princes, came to help me, for I had been left there
with the kings of Persia.*

—Dan. 10:13

Our target for this section was merely to find out what they
looked like, right? Let's get those tallies.

Cherubim	wings, hands, able to be ridden, and an ox face	Guards/ mounts
Seraphim	6 wings, hands, talks . . . a lot Face and feet are *covered* by wings	Court bailiff
Archangel	Looks like a man, may cause fear	Guards against Satan
Angel	Looks like a man, may cause fear	Messenger

*For in the resurrection they neither marry nor are given
in marriage, but are like angels in heaven.*

—Matt. 22:30

In Luke 20 we see they cannot die.

*Jesus said to them, "The sons of this age marry and are
given in marriage, but those who are considered worthy
to attain to that age and the resurrection from the dead,
neither marry nor are given in marriage; for they cannot
even die anymore, because they are like angels, and are
sons of God, being sons of the resurrection.*

—Luke 20:34–36

Cherubim	wings, hands, able to be ridden, and an ox face	Guards/ mounts
Seraphim	6 wings, hands, talks . . . a lot Face and feet are *covered* by wings	Court bailiff
Archangel	Looks like a man, may cause fear, cannot die, no marriage	Guards against Satan
Angel	Looks like a man, may cause fear, cannot die, no marriage	Messenger

Then I saw an angel coming down from heaven, holding the key of the abyss and a great chain in his hand. And he laid hold of the dragon, the serpent of old, who is the devil and Satan, and bound him for a thousand years; and he threw him into the abyss, and shut it and sealed it over him, so that he would not deceive the nations any longer, until the thousand years were completed; after these things he must be released for a short time.

—Rev. 20:1–3

Christ defeated death and sin. Michael seems to be the one who is aimed at Satan and battle. Throwing him down seems reasonable to assume he is the jailer too. It's just a theory and not proven.

What do normal angels look like?

People.

Now the two angels came to Sodom in the evening as Lot was sitting in the gate of Sodom. When Lot saw them, he rose to meet them and bowed down with his face to the ground.

—Gen. 19:1

There was a "shining" or reverence that Lot recognized before he even spoke to these angels.

But the evil townsfolk . . .

And they called to Lot and said to him, "Where are the men who came to you tonight? Bring them out to us that we may have relations with them."

—Gen. 19:5

The evil townsfolk desired them, in the biblical way.

The angel of the Lord appeared to him in a blazing fire from the midst of a bush; and he looked, and behold, the bush was burning with fire, yet the bush was not consumed.

—Exod. 3:2

Do not neglect to show hospitality to strangers, for by this some have entertained angels without knowing it.

—Heb. 13:2

And behold, a severe earthquake had occurred, for an angel of the Lord descended from heaven and came and rolled away the stone and sat upon it. And his appearance was like lightning, and his clothing as white as snow. The guards shook for fear of him and became like dead men.

—Matt. 28:2–4

All these verses provide evidence that regular angels can appear as beautiful, as terrible, as a fiery bush, and even as a snake.

Now the serpent was more crafty than any beast of the field which the Lord God had made. And he said to the woman, "Indeed, has God said, 'You shall not eat from any tree of the garden'?"

—Gen. 3:1

And the great dragon was thrown down, the serpent of old who is called the devil and Satan, who deceives the whole world; he was thrown down to the earth, and his angels were thrown down with him.

—Rev. 12:9

But was Satan an angel?

How you have fallen from heaven,
O star of the morning, son of the dawn!
You have been cut down to the earth,
You who have weakened the nations!

—Isa. 14:12

You were in Eden, the garden of God;
Every precious stone was your covering:
The ruby, the topaz and the diamond;
The beryl, the onyx and the jasper;
The lapis lazuli, the turquoise and the emerald;
And the gold, the workmanship of your settings and sockets,
Was in you.
On the day that you were created

They were prepared.
You were the anointed cherub who covers,
And I placed you there.
You were on the holy mountain of God;
You walked in the midst of the stones of fire.
You were blameless in your ways
From the day you were created Until unrighteousness
was found in you.
By the abundance of your trade
You were internally filled with violence,
And you sinned;
Therefore I have cast you as profane
From the mountain of God.
And I have destroyed you, O covering cherub,
From the midst of the stones of fire.
Your heart was lifted up because of your beauty;
You corrupted your wisdom by reason of your splendor.
I cast you to the ground;
I put you before kings,
That they may see you.
By the multitude of your iniquities,
In the unrighteousness of your trade
You profaned your sanctuaries.
Therefore I have brought fire from the midst of you;
It has consumed you,
And I have turned you to ashes on the earth
In the eyes of all who see you.
All who know you among the peoples
Are appalled at you;
You have become terrified
And you will cease to be forever.

—Ezek. 28:13–19

Satan was a cherub. He was a guard over mankind, and he changed himself to become a snake to seduce mankind (my opinion is that the term *serpent* was added to him as a dirt slitherer due to his transgressions, *but* I will break this down far better in another book in a chapter called "Garden of Eden").

The Bible point-blank identifies Satan as a cherub with the face of a *bull*, at least before God cursed him. Could the cursing have left him in his original form and been more of a metaphor? Sure.

Let's answer some more of those ideas we addressed at the very beginning.

Angels have wings and halos and play musical instruments. They're kind of like God's backup singers, and they look like babies.

I think we definitely proved, using the Bible, that this is *not* what angels look like. Hallmark or a movie or TV show has imbedded that thought into our culture. It is against Scripture, and that thought needs to perish.

Angels are sitting on our shoulders and looking out for us. Each of us has a personal guardian angel who keeps us out of trouble.

Behold, I am going to send an angel before you to guard you along the way and to bring you into the place which I have prepared.

—Exod. 23:20

No, God does not permanently assign his angels to "accident prevention." There may be a single event or a small period of time that he does dispatch an angel, especially for the entire flock of his children, but in his history book, he does not do this personal guardian angel thing. This is literally the Exodus, as in the fleeing of the *entire* tribe of Hebrews escaping from Egypt. If you believe we all have a guardian angel, please tell me where in the Bible you get that. Or are you just making up a new religion?

Angels are amazing beings who want us to be happy.

No, angels obey the commands they are given—nothing more, nothing less. Gabriel feels genuinely nice, but Michael treated Joshua with coldness—a matter-of-factness. I hesitate to use the word *disgust* or *agitation*, but the fact that he had his sword out says something. I'm not sure what it was, but it didn't feel warm and fuzzy.

Angels are better than humans in some way.

They do possess different abilities, but better?

They struck the men who were at the doorway of the house with blindness, both small and great, so that they wearied themselves trying to find the doorway.

—Gen. 19:11

They can strike men blind, but can they procreate?

They can morph their bodies into various shapes and beauties, but do they have an earthly time to run wild before coming into the fold of God as humans do?

Matthew 1:20 tells us they can appear in our dreams, but can they feel the urgency of death chasing them? Do they have the drive of life that we have, knowing that an end is coming? Do they feel the bittersweetness of mortality?

Were the fallen angels offered redemption? No, because they had sight. They *knew* God was there and still rebelled, at least some of them. In my opinion, we are being handled with kid gloves at this moment. The angels never were.

123

People become angels when they die.

Now at that time Michael, the great prince who stands guard over the sons of your people, will arise. And there will be a time of distress such as never occurred since there was a nation until that time; and at that time your people, everyone who is found written in the book, will be rescued. Many of those who sleep in the dust of the ground will awake, these to everlasting life, but the others to disgrace and everlasting contempt. Those who have insight will shine brightly like the brightness of the expanse of heaven, and those who lead the many to righteousness, like the stars forever and ever. But as for you, Daniel, conceal these words and seal up the book until the end of time; many will go back and forth, and knowledge will increase.

—Dan. 12:1–4

No, people do not become angels when they die.

People die and go to sleep to await judgment. They're *not* in purgatory. They're not angelic bodies. They're not guardian angels. It's not "I know Uncle Roy is up there watching over us all." It's not "I know Grandma is probably playing hearts (the card game) up there right now."

Sleep. Everyone who has died since the flood of Noah's time is A-S-L-E-E-P. Maybe a single person here and there has been pulled by God for a specific reason, but 99.99999 percent of everyone who dies goes to *sleep.*

But we do not want you to be uninformed, brethren, about those who are asleep, so that you will not grieve as do the rest who have no hope. For if we believe that Jesus died and rose again, even so God will bring with Him those who have fallen asleep in Jesus. For this we say to you by the word of the Lord, that we who are alive and remain until the coming of the Lord, will not precede those who have fallen asleep. For the Lord Himself will descend from heaven with a shout, with the voice of the archangel and with the trumpet of God, and the dead in Christ will rise first. Then we who are alive and remain will be caught up together with them in the clouds to meet the Lord in the air, and so we shall always be with the Lord. Therefore comfort one another with these words.

—1 Thess. 4:13–18

This is talking about Christ's second return to earth, the Revelation period. The people who are no longer drawing breath are *asleep.*

I am sorry, my congregation. I am sorry. I have heard a ton of songs talking about "Grandpa looking down," "Momma is watching," or "heaven got another angel." These statements are not true if you call yourself a Christian. I know they may bring a sort of comfort, but we were called to be *truthful* before comforting. We cannot and must not continue speaking lies and allowing them to circulate around us.

The dead are asleep. They are resting until they are called by God.

Angels know everything.

In whatever our heart condemns us; for God is greater than our heart and knows all things.

—1 John 3:20

Angels are not God. God alone knows everything.

My family, I know this book may feel like Glen is ripping apart your world. I feel the pain of that, even as I sit here typing this. I am sorry. I smell your confusion. I taste your mind struggling to release the teachings of your whole life and embrace the true teachings of the Bible. This book takes some very hard whacks at common knowledge and practices that the Bible says you shouldn't believe or do.

You are not alone. Take your struggles to your homegroup. Take it to the church. Take it to your elders. Let them help you if they are in line with the Bible.

In the great state of Texas, we have a saying: "I'd rather be judged by 12 than carried by 6." This is a bolstered way of saying I would rather be judged for shooting someone who breaks into my home than hesitate and get killed. This statement was written into my fiber when I was just a child, *but* this is *not* a Christian statement, and I have had to let it go. If someone breaks into my home, I need to assess the situation properly and be ready for immediate action, up to and including defending my life. Before my fellow rednecks get all "pitch-forky," imagine this: the kid next door is a 12-year-old mentally handicapped boy who sneaks out of his house and breaks into yours. And you, without confronting the intruder, shoot your weapon at the intruder. It is not about being judged by 12. It is about my being able to live with the thought that I killed an innocent person.

Cling to the Bible, or cling to the world. Your God has given you the choice by giving you free will.

Angels are not supreme beings. They are letter carriers, prison guards, and court bailiffs. A few (one) are in charge of battling a specific entity.

Do not praise the pizza delivery person for the tasty pizza.

126

Recognize them for not taking 75 minutes to complete a 15-minute drive to your house. Recognize them for the hard work of delivering pizza, but never kneel to them. Angels are not God. They are not your relatives who come back to life. They are also not babies.

They are entities running all over the earth doing what God tells them to do—nothing more, nothing less.

I will leave you with this last fact from the Bible.

According to the book of Revelation:

Then I looked, and I heard the voice of many angels around the throne and the living creatures and the elders; and the number of them was myriads of myriads, and thousands of thousands,

—Rev. 5:11

The King James Version captures this as "ten thousand times ten thousand, and thousands of thousands" (Rev. 5:11 KJV).

There is a heavenly host up above and all around, and they are running all over the earth and reporting back to the Father.

When Satan gets in the way, Michael comes down. That's why Satan had to make a deal with God before he went after Job in the Old Testament. Satan couldn't directly target Job because that is not within an angel's or a cherub's power. Also, bull-boy doesn't want another Michael-sized butt-whooping. Satan whispers. Satan questions, just like he did to Eve and Jesus. Only when God granted him the power to harass Job did Satan do those things.

Our God is stronger, our heavenly army is stronger, and our faith is stronger than the hate of the darkness.

Love each other, for many of us have entertained angels and have not even known it.

P.S. Angels are also referred to as "watchers" and "holy ones."

IS HARRY POTTER EVIL?

The title of this chapter is the main opinion of the people who form the tip of the spear of this school of thought. Let me explain.

Harry Potter is a story about a boy whose parents died, and he is treated badly by his guardian aunt and uncle. Young Harry receives a letter inviting him to attend the same school of magic that his parents attended. He finds out that magic is real and that his selfish guardians have lied to him. Harry goes to the school of magic, and under what can be easily classified as negligent supervision by adults, he learns to use magic. The real story is about the boy and his friends defeating the dark side of magic and its users. These books by J. K. Rowling are children's books.

When the first book came out, it was quickly turned into a movie, and a Christian forest fire was lit. Church after church condemned this book and movie because it embraced witchcraft.

If the Bible is true, then that means magic is real.

Then Pharaoh also called for the wise men and the sorcerers, and they also, the magicians of Egypt, did the same with their secret arts. For each one threw down his staff and they turned into serpents.

—Exod. 7:11–12

If the Bible is true, God uses magic too.

*Now the Lord **spoke to Moses and Aaron**, saying, "When Pharaoh speaks to you, saying, 'Work a miracle,' then you shall say to Aaron, 'Take your staff and throw it down before Pharaoh, that it may become a serpent.'" So Moses and Aaron came to Pharaoh, and thus they did just as the Lord had commanded; and Aaron threw his staff down before Pharaoh and his servants, and it became a serpent.*

—Exod. 7:8–10

God and his servants use magic all the time.

So the sun stood still, and the moon stopped,

Until the nation avenged themselves of their enemies.

Is it not written in the book of Jashar? And the sun stopped in the middle of the sky and did not hasten to go down for about a whole day. There was no day like that before it or after it, when the Lord listened to the voice of a man; for the Lord fought for Israel.

—Josh.10:13–14

Stopping the sun from moving sounds magical to me.

Then Moses stretched out his hand over the sea; and the Lord swept the sea back by a strong east wind all night and turned the sea into dry land, so the waters were divided.

—Exod. 14:21

Using wind to hold back water—that's kind of like Dr. Strange did during the battle in the movie *Avengers: End Game*. Yup, Dr. Strange was a wizard who used magic too.

So Aaron stretched out his hand over the waters of Egypt, and the frogs came up and covered the land of Egypt. The magicians did the same with their secret arts, making frogs come up on the land of Egypt.

—Exod. 8:6–7

A plague of frogs—one of the Jedi powers in *Star Wars* is "animal bond." Obi-Wan Kenobi was great at it, which is why he was able to ride mounts so easily and calm the beast that was attacking him at Geonosis. These were space wizards using magic.

The tombs were opened, and many bodies of the saints who had fallen asleep were raised; and coming out of the tombs after His resurrection they entered the holy city and appeared to many.

—Matt. 27:52–53

Necromancy. Yes, there is a *Necromancer* video game called *Skyrim* where one of the magical abilities is to raise the dead, but only for a little while.

Now the centurion, and those who were with him keeping guard over Jesus, when they saw the earthquake and the things that were happening, became very frightened and said, "Truly this was the Son of God!"

—Matt. 27:54

Magical earthquakes? Sure. In the game *Dungeons & Dragons*, there is a magical spell called "earthquake," and it causes . . . earthquakes.

> *And the Lord opened the mouth of the donkey, and she said to Balaam, "What have I done to you, that you have struck me these three times?"*
>
> —Num. 22:28

Animals talking? I remember Harry Potter having a conversation with a snake.

> *Then the Lord rained on Sodom and Gomorrah brimstone and fire from the Lord out of heaven.*
>
> —Gen. 19:24

I remember Thanos in *Avengers: Infinity War* using magic gems to drop fragments of a moon on people.

> *They struck the men who were at the doorway of the house with blindness, both small and great, so that they wearied themselves trying to find the doorway.*
>
> —Gen. 19:11

Harry Potter again—that spell is called Obscuro.

> *They said to Him, "We have here only five loaves and two fish." And He said, "Bring them here to Me." Ordering the people to sit down on the grass, He took the five loaves and the two fish, and looking up toward heaven, He blessed the food, and breaking the loaves He gave them*

to the disciples, and the disciples gave them to the crowds, and they all ate and were satisfied. They picked up what was leftover of the broken pieces, twelve full baskets. There were about five thousand men who ate, besides women and children.

—Matt. 14:17–21

That is conjuration.

But when he had considered this, behold, an angel of the Lord appeared to him in a dream, saying, "Joseph, son of David, do not be afraid to take Mary as your wife; for the Child who has been conceived in her is of the Holy Spirit."

—Matt. 1:20

Yup, that's called dream walking. Magic too.

Magic is real. When it is God's magic, we call it a miracle. When it is not of God, we call it magic. It is the *same thing* but from different sources.

Let me change gears for just a second.

If this line of thinking is troubling you, I have one or two questions for you.

Why are you so prejudiced?

or

Why are you so lazy?

You see, we as biblical Christians know that miracles and magic are real.

Now there are varieties of gifts, but the same Spirit. And there are varieties of ministries, and the same Lord.

There are varieties of effects, but the same God who works all things in all persons. But to each one is given the manifestation of the Spirit for the common good. For to one is given the word of wisdom through the Spirit, and to another the word of knowledge according to the same Spirit; to another faith by the same Spirit, and to another gifts of healing by the one Spirit, and to another the effecting of miracles, and to another prophecy, and to another the distinguishing of spirits, to another various kinds of tongues, and to another the interpretation of tongues. But one and the same Spirit works all these things, distributing to each one individually just as He wills.

—1 Cor. 12:4–11

Many will say to Me on that day, 'Lord, Lord, did we not prophesy in Your name, and in Your name cast out demons, and in Your name perform many miracles?' And then I will declare to them, 'I never knew you; depart from Me, you who practice lawlessness.'"

—Matt. 7:22–23

There is magic from God and magic *not* from God. We as an entire religion have taken anything that looks like magic and thrown it into a blasphemy prison, yet most people who are not of the Abrahamic religions (Jew, Christian, Muslim) who read our book or hear our stories say "magic."

So when you—someone who has a God who has performed deeds that the secular world calls magic—deny that magic exists, you make yourself a liar.

When you tell me you follow Christ, the being who

performed a magical act that transformed two loaves of bread into a whole lot more, you make yourself a liar.

This is prejudice against a word. It makes no sense.

Glen, we are talking about *non*-godly magic. That is why we condemned *Harry Potter* movies.

Okay, but why stop there?

Gimme some rope, ya'll, cause we're gonna get real.

Is lying a sin?

Yes.

What about lying for money?

Yes.

But what if I give you a bunch of money to tell a lie?

Yes, Glen, it is still a lie.

But what if I give you a bunch of money, put a movie camera in front of you, and have a director say "action"? Is that lie you are telling still a lie? Is that a sin?

What if we write a script that glorifies God, hire only Christians to work on the film, give all the proceeds to the church, and pray every day before we start filming? Would that actor still be a liar and sinning?

Family, when you apply the actual logic of the Holy Spirit to your socially accepted prejudices, things look very different.

A lie is a lie regardless of who pays you what and what your intentions are.

Church, if we throw *Harry Potter* out because of witchcraft, we also throw out all movies and TV where anyone plays a role that is not their actual person.

Law and Order—*gone.*

Movies—*gone.*

Christian movies about Christ—*gone.*

Oh, we don't just stop there.

Do you know that cute Christmas play the children's

department puts on each year where they dress up as Mary and Joseph and read lines of the nativity scene? You know, the one where little Tommy gets up and says, "I am Joseph," and little Billy makes a frumpy face and says, "There is no room in the inn."

Oops! He is pretending, and pretending is a lie.

All right, Glen, can't we just have the kids stand there and not read lines?

Nope. When the kids dress up, they're pretending to be someone else, and that is a deception and against the Bible.

Here are some more things that need to go.

Dressing kids up for trick-or-treating—*gone.*

Dressing up as a pilgrim or a Native American for a Thanksgiving play—*gone.*

Having Grandpa dress up as Santa for Christmas and going to the orphanage to hand out free toys—*gone.*

Ya'll get it yet?

When you pull the string of entertainment, almost every bit of it comes loose. All forms of entertainment that involve *any* area of make-believe become blasphemy.

Are you a Christian?

Do you have the Holy Spirit in you?

When you act or pretend, will you be verbalizing a non-truth?

Is lying a sin?

Blasphemy!

Intense, huh? That section was for the prejudiced. Now let's go after the lazy, which I think most of us are. I believe we verbalize prejudiced views out of laziness.

Bros and Mos, I give you this *one* single direction. Learn discernment. Learn to know what is right versus wrong according to God and the Bible. Learn this.

Chris Cagle sings an amazing song called "Let There Be Cowgirls." I love this song—the tempo, the twang, the story. I love how it lifts our boot-wearing mamas to their proper height; I love how it is strong and salty. In this song, Chris starts with the creation story from Genesis, but he gets things out of order very quickly. For the longest time, I secretly loved this song but refused to listen to it because it was biblically incorrect.

Discernment. It is a good song even if it got things a little out of order.

We are all dirty with sin. Everything we touch has a tiny bit of sin on it because we are covered in sin.

Family, please learn to discern what is of God versus what is not. Teach your children to do the same. Don't be afraid to have a conversation with them.

But Glen, I have a responsibility to protect my children from these dark influences.

Really? Do you think it is possible to be the crops mixed with the weeds and keep your people separate? You are not protecting them; you are isolating them because running a prison house is easier than running a schoolhouse.

Do you think I am crazy? Why do you think the idea of a 22-year-old virgin Christian is almost a myth today? Arguably, 70 percent of America claims to be Christians. Do you think 70 percent of Christian college kids are virgins? Were you a virgin when you met your spouse, Mr. and Mrs. Lazy Christian?

Your kids *will* be exposed to the darkness. All you are doing is passing the teaching of discernment on to someone else.

Let me be clear. The darkness can't wait for your innocent, sheltered, naive, 18-year-old *adult* to go to college, join the military, or move out of your house. The darkness is drooling at the thought of feasting on your child. Your tactic of confinement and isolation is a failing one. This has been proven time and again by statistics. Some will hold firm, but not many.

Hey, just for fun, does anyone want to guess the average age of exotic dancers? It is 23.5 years old.

Teach your children to discern, *not* just obey.

Watch movies with them, and then discuss them. Watch *Harry Potter* with them. In the end, explain that the story was good and Harry had a strong will that allowed him to put away the lies of his aunt and uncle and embrace what he felt he needed to do. Also talk about the use of magic and that when supernatural powers come from God, it is a miracle. Then ask them where Harry got his magic from. He didn't get it from God. Take this opportunity to show them the story of Moses and how Aaron and Moses had to deal with magicians too.

Discernment. Teach them.

Play video games with them. Listen to music with them. Get into what they are into so you can teach them.

Parenting is about the child, right? *Right?* Put some real effort into this. They are young only once.

When my son was nine-ish, he wanted to be a Marine, just like Daddy. Camo, salutes, and Nerf guns became his norm. It reached a point where I felt like he went past childish pretending and was starting to idolize and romanticize being a soldier. Being a soldier can be terrifying. Then the movie *Fury* came out starring Brad Pitt. I did all the research, read the reviews, and made sure this was a tool fit for the job I had planned. I expected violence and bad language, but nothing else according to the reviews.

My son and I devised a plan.

If things got too intense for him, he would cover his eyes and look down, and then I would put my hands over his ears until the scene changed. If I thought something was too inappropriate, I would cover his ears, and he would immediately look down. My boy and I had our plan, and the ticket person thought I was crazy.

We went, and we watched. He spent a fourth of the movie on my lap, ears covered and looking down. It was rough, and when we walked out, the first thing he asked was, "Daddy, do Marines cuss that much?"

"Yes, my son, many of us do."

Indeed, it was brutal, but he got a good taste of the immense brutality that can come from warfare.

"Daddy, did you do those things too?"

"No, son, I was in the air wing. We made airplanes fly. But I wanted you to see a worst-case scenario if everything went wrong. I wanted you to see what life as a soldier could be like."

I wanted him to understand what the term *Medal of Honor* meant and what some of those people had to endure to earn that award.

My son hugged me. He still wants to be a Marine, but he doesn't want to drive a tank.

I told him that if he ever did join the Marine Corps, it would be a proud and a sad day for me—proud because he followed in my footsteps and decided to serve in the military for his country and sad because I know the things he will have to endure, even if he doesn't go 0311 Infantry. I knew the temptations and influences he would have to resist. I told him that one day this would be his choice, and no matter what he chose, I still love him and would be proud of him. I want him to have full knowledge of how bad things can get before he raises his right hand and swears to defend our country. Four years later, he still wants to be a Marine. I failed at trying to lure him away from Uncle Sam's Misguided Children (USMC), but he stopped idolizing warfare, and that was my real goal.

We talked at length for about an hour after the movie. We shared words about everything he saw and how it made him feel. We discussed Christ and turning the other cheek. We discussed buying a sword.

> *And He said to them, "But now, whoever has a money belt is to take it along, likewise also a bag, and whoever has no sword is to sell his coat and buy one.*
>
> —Luke 22:36

A sword is used only for one purpose, and it isn't hunting.

You can run in fear every time you hear the word *magic*, but remember this:

> *Now after Jesus was born in Bethlehem of Judea in the days of Herod the king, magi from the east arrived in Jerusalem, saying, "Where is He who has been born King of the Jews? For we saw His star in the east and have come to worship Him."*
>
> —Matt. 2:1–2

Those three "wise men" who brought gifts to the baby Jesus were magi. *Magi*—like magicians, like magic. Look in the Greek. It's the same word. Magi = magus = magos.

Be careful what you consider to be blasphemy because you might just be condemning the servants of God.

There is good magic from God. Everything else is not good. Witchcraft is *not* good.

Sidenote: Talking to dead people is never okay. They are asleep, so let them sleep. Most of the time you are just talking to a demon who hitched a ride with that person during their lifetime, but that is pulling a curtain back that many of you aren't ready for.

Moving on . . .

There is a third group of people I just cannot find fault with regarding throwing out all entertainment. That is a group I will call "minimalists." Pretty much if it is not necessary, it is not embraced. Movies are not necessary—*gone*. The National Football League—*gone*. Television—*gone*. Radio—*gone*. Kids sports with little girls in skimpy "athletic" clothing—*gone*. Pretty much if it is not necessary for life, it is gone.

These people tend to have large properties and live self-sufficient lives. This sounds boring, and it might be closer to Christ's wants than the world's sinful desires, but there is one glaring problem. We are called to grow among the weeds. We were called to show the world the light. It is hard to do that when you have withdrawn from the world. I genuinely desire this existence—my wife and my kids just living on a large piece of property—but the Bible doesn't teach that.

The way I see it, you have two real options. Call all pretending as lying sin and outlaw any form of it from your world, or teach your children to discern the Word of God versus the world, God's magic from bad magic.

P.S. Do *not* take your child to see the movie *Fury*. It was far rougher than I had intended and poor, poor discernment on my behalf.

Hacksaw Ridge directed by Mel Gibson is dramatically

better and shows a much more beautiful message about being in war, doing your part, but not causing death. It is a true story about the first conscientious objector in World War II. Read his Medal of Honor citation, and tell me this man wasn't completely powered by the will of our God.

Love you, Desmond Doss. Rest up, Doc, you earned it.

WHO WROTE WHAT?

Who wrote what books of the Bible? It's pretty simple.

Old Testament		
Genesis	Moses	
Exodus	Moses	
Leviticus	Moses	AKA Torah
Numbers	Moses	
Deuteronomy	Moses	
Joshua	Unknown	
Judges	Unknown	
Ruth	Unknown	
1 Samuel	Unknown	
2 Samuel	Unknown	
1 Kings	Unknown	
1 Kings	Unknown	
1 Chronicles	Ezra	
2 Chronicles	Ezra	
Ezra	Ezra	
Nehemiah	Nehemiah	
Esther	Unknown	
Job	Unknown	

Psalms	David: 73 Asaph: 12 Sons of Korah: 11 Solomon: 2 Moses: 1 Ethan: 1 Heman: 1 Unknown: 50	
Proverbs	Solomon: 29 Agur: 1 Lemuel: 1	
Ecclesiastes	Solomon	
Song of Solomon	Solomon	
Isaiah	Isaiah	Major Prophet
Jeremiah	Jeremiah	Major Prophet
Lamentations	Jeremiah	
Ezekiel	Ezekiel	Major Prophet
Daniel	Daniel	Major Prophet
Hosea	Hosea	Minor Prophet
Joel	Joel	Minor Prophet
Amos	Amos	Minor Prophet
Obadiah	Obadiah	Minor Prophet
Jonah	Jonah	Minor Prophet
Micah	Micah	Minor Prophet
Nahum	Nahum	Minor Prophet
Habakkuk	Habakkuk	Minor Prophet
Zephaniah	Zephaniah	Minor Prophet
Haggai	Haggai	Minor Prophet
Zechariah	Zechariah	Minor Prophet
Malachi	Malachi	Minor Prophet

New Testament	
Matthew	Matthew
Mark	John Mark
Luke	Luke
John	John
Acts	Luke
Romans	Paul
1 Corinthians	Paul
2 Corinthians	Paul
Galatians	Paul
Ephesians	Paul
Philippians	Paul
Colossians	Paul
1 Thessalonians	Paul
2 Thessalonians	Paul
1 Timothy	Paul
2 Timothy	Paul
Titus	Paul
Philemon	Paul
Hebrews	Unknown
James	James (Jesus's brother)
1 Peter	Peter
2 Peter	Peter
1 John	John
2 John	John
3 John	John
Jude	Jude
Revelation	John

Remember, part of this book is intended for reference.

12 TRIBES

Why is this important?

It helps make the connection between early Genesis Hebrews and the modern-day Jewish religion.

These are God's children, the second invited to the feast, so it might be good to know a little about them.

The end times will have a recalling of the 144,000, which are of the 12 tribes. Israel is not out of God's ball game yet.

Most importantly, there are a couple of verses that sound strange unless you understand who the 12 tribes are. The next chapter in this book will open that up.

The origin of the 12 tribes was Abram. God made Abram a promise and then changed his name to Abraham.

Abram fell on his face, and God talked with him, saying,
"As for Me, behold, My covenant is with you,
And you will be the father of a multitude of nations.
No longer shall your name be called Abram,
But your name shall be Abraham;
For I have made you the father of a multitude of nations.

"I will make you exceedingly fruitful, and I will make
nations of you, and kings will come forth from you. I will

establish My covenant between Me and you and your descendants after you throughout their generations for an everlasting covenant, to be God to you and to your descendants after you. I will give to you and to your descendants after you, the land of your sojournings, all the land of Canaan, for an everlasting possession; and I will be their God.

—Gen. 17:3–8

Abraham had Isaac.

Isaac had Jacob (aka Israel).

Jacob had children with four women, wives, and concubines. The story of how all this happened was crazy. Start reading at Genesis 29:15. Leah was his first wife; Rachel was his second. Bilhah and Zilpah were his wife's handmaidens turned concubines because of Rachel's jealousy of Leah, her elder sister. All the while Jacob only desired Rachel. Leah came back into the picture and had two more kids because Rachel wanted mandrake—for real. This is tabloid magazine stuff.

The kids' births were like this:

1	Leah	Reuben	7	Zilpah	Gad
2	Leah	Simeon	8	Zilpah	Asher
3	Leah	Levi	9	Leah	Issachar
4	Leah	Judah	10	Leah	Zebulun
5	Bilhah	Dan	11	Rachel	Joseph
6	Bilhah	Naphtali	12	Rachel	Benjamin

Gather together and hear, O sons of Jacob;
And listen to Israel your father.
Reuben, you are my firstborn;
My might and the beginning of my strength,
Preeminent in dignity and preeminent in power.
Uncontrolled as water, you shall not have preeminence,
Because you went up to your father's bed;
Then you defiled it—he went up to my couch.

—Gen. 49:2–4

Remember the curse of Canaan from *Enough Chaos Volume 1*? Yup. It happened again.

Look at Genesis 35:22 when you have time. We are continuing.

Simeon and Levi are brothers;
Their swords are implements of violence.
Let my soul not enter into their council;
Let not my glory be united with their assembly;
Because in their anger they slew men,
And in their self-will they lamed oxen.
Cursed be their anger, for it is fierce;
And their wrath, for it is cruel.
I will disperse them in Jacob,
And scatter them in Israel.
Judah, your brothers shall praise you;
Your hand shall be on the neck of your enemies;
Your father's sons shall bow down to you.
Judah is a lion's whelp;
From the prey, my son, you have gone up.
He couches, he lies down as a lion,

And as a lion, who dares rouse him up?
The scepter shall not depart from Judah,
Nor the ruler's staff from between his feet,
Until Shiloh comes,
And to him shall be the obedience of the peoples.
He ties his foal to the vine,
And his donkey's colt to the choice vine;
He washes his garments in wine,
And his robes in the blood of grapes.
His eyes are dull from wine,
And his teeth white from milk.
Zebulun will dwell at the seashore;
And he shall be a haven for ships,
And his flank shall be toward Sidon.
Issachar is a strong donkey,
Lying down between the sheepfolds.
When he saw that a resting place was good
And that the land was pleasant,
He bowed his shoulder to bear burdens,
And became a slave at forced labor.
Dan shall judge his people,
As one of the tribes of Israel.
Dan shall be a serpent in the way,
A horned snake in the path,
That bites the horse's heels,
So that his rider falls backward.
For Your salvation I wait, O Lord.
As for Gad, raiders shall raid him,
But he will raid at their heels.
As for Asher, his food shall be rich,
And he will yield royal dainties.
Naphtali is a doe let loose,

He gives beautiful words.
Joseph is a fruitful bough,
A fruitful bough by a spring;
Its branches run over a wall.
The archers bitterly attacked him,
And shot at him and harassed him;
But his bow remained firm,
And his arms were agile,
From the hands of the Mighty One of Jacob
(From there is the Shepherd, the Stone of Israel),
From the God of your father who helps you,
And by the Almighty who blesses you
With blessings of heaven above,
Blessings of the deep that lies beneath,
Blessings of the breasts and of the womb.
The blessings of your father
Have surpassed the blessings of my ancestors
Up to the utmost bound of the everlasting hills; May they
be on the head of Joseph,
And on the crown of the head of the one distinguished
among his brothers.
Benjamin is a ravenous wolf;
In the morning he devours the prey,
And in the evening he divides the spoil.

—Gen. 49:5–27

To wrap all that up:

1	**Reuben**	water
2	**Simeon**	swords
3	**Levi**	swords

4	Judah	lion's whelp, scepter shall not depart until Shiloh comes (Shiloh means peace/rest)
5	Zebulun	ships
6	Issachar	strong donkey
7	Dan	judge his people
8	Gad	he will raid
9	Asher	food shall be rich
10	Naphtali	doe let loose
11	Joseph	fruitful bough
12	Benjamin	ravenous wolf

When you cross the Jordan, these shall stand on Mount Gerizim to bless the people: Simeon, Levi, Judah, Issachar, Joseph, and Benjamin. For the curse, these shall stand on Mount Ebal: Reuben, Gad, Asher, Zebulun, Dan, and Naphtali.

—Deut. 27:12–13

The tribes that had openly committed sins were considered cursed and got the barren land to dwell in.

Here are the cursed:

Reuben	Gad	Asher	Zebulun	Dan	Naphtali

Reuben was creepy and cursed.

Dan, Naphtali, Gad, and Asher were all mothered by concubines.

1	Leah	Reuben		7	Zilpah	Gad
2				8	Zilpah	Asher
3				9		
4				10	Leah	Zebulun
5	Bilhah	Dan		11		
6	Bilhah	Naphtali		12		

But what about Zebulun?

Family, I have no clue.

Some people will try to say it is because of Judges 1:30. Zebulun failed to drive out the inhabitants, but that was in Joshua's time, later. Why the curse at this time in the story?

Other people say he was the youngest of Leah's sons and wanted to make the inhabitants equal, but that is a strange point to make. I could see Benjamin because he was the youngest of the kids, but pointing out the first wife's last child is strange. Unless all the brothers knew that Rachel was the favored wife, Leah was the least and Zebulun was the youngest of the least favorite.

I'm not buying that, but it is the least crazy theory.

Let's face it, folks. Everything about Jacob's wives and kids is crazy. This silliness is not the silliest thing in this story.

Moving on!

The 12 tribes dwelled, spread out, waged war, and become the land of Israel, taking their father's God-given name. There was a lot of fighting, both with outsiders and especially within the tribes themselves, and eventually, they broke into two nations. Ten tribes formed the northern kingdom, and two tribes formed the southern kingdom. The north was defeated by the Assyrians and exiled. If you hear the term "the lost tribes" or "the lost 10," these are who they are talking about.

The southern kingdom, which includes the city of Jerusalem, was attacked a lot by all kinds of people, including Egyptians, Philistines, Arabians, Ethiopians, and Syrians. Finally, the southern kingdom was defeated by the Babylonians. These two tribes were Judah and Benjamin, but the tribe of Levi had cities (not land) (Josh. 14:4), so there were also Levite cities in the southern kingdom.

During this Babylonian captivity, Benjamin and Levi were fully absorbed into Judah. Then the Persians came in and took over. Then Alexander the Great defeated Persia and was the new ruler. Then Alex died, and Ptolemy I took over and lost Jerusalem to the Seleucids. Jewish rebels took control of the city for 103 years (known as the Hasmonean Period). Near the end of this period, two brothers argued and asked Rome to intervene, and thus it became a province of Rome. finally . . . finally . . . in 37 BCE, Herod the Great (yes, *that* Herod) captured Jerusalem and ruled as a client king of Rome. It may come to some of our minds that these people were God's children. How could he do that to them?

"Are you not as the sons of Ethiopia to Me,
O sons of Israel?" declares the Lord.
"Have I not brought up Israel from the land of Egypt,
And the Philistines from Caphtor and the Arameans
from Kir?
Behold, the eyes of the Lord God are on the sinful
kingdom,
And I will destroy it from the face of the earth;
Nevertheless, I will not totally destroy the house of Jacob,"
Declares the Lord.
"For behold, I am commanding,
And I will shake the house of Israel among all nations

As grain is shaken in a sieve,
But not a kernel will fall to the ground.
All the sinners of My people will die by the sword,
Those who say, 'The calamity will not overtake or
confront us.'"

—Amos 9:7–10

The tribes were warned time and again—again, and again, and again. They were warned. They were warned by their dad, Jacob. They were warned a bazillion times. They never held firm to God as a tribe, and thus they were ruined.

Even under Roman rule, the Jewish leaders were just nasty, corrupt, and greedy, so much so that they pushed for the crucifixion of Christ. They were warned what was coming, and they refused to listen even when Christ himself came and told them.

Again, moving on!

Church, if you look at all the places the 12 tribes are listed, you will find a handful of issues. Tribes' names get removed, and all of a sudden Manasseh and Ephraim get added. These are not errors.

The original 12 tribes are recorded in Genesis 35:22–26, 49:3–27, Exodus 1:2–5, Deuteronomy 27:12–13, and 1 Chronicles 2:1, but something did happen in Genesis 48 that explains the differences.

Now it came about after these things that Joseph was told, "Behold, your father is sick." So he took his two sons Manasseh and Ephraim with him. When it was told to Jacob, "Behold, your son Joseph has come to you," Israel collected his strength and sat up in the bed. Then Jacob said to Joseph, "God Almighty appeared to me at Luz in the land of Canaan and blessed me, and He said to me, 'Behold, I will make you fruitful and numerous, and I will make you a company of peoples, and will give this land to your descendants after you for an everlasting possession.' Now your two sons, who were born to you in the land of Egypt before I came to you in Egypt, are mine; Ephraim and Manasseh shall be mine, as Reuben and Simeon are.

—Gen. 48:1–5

God himself blessed Joseph, so Jacob passed his blessing from Joseph to his two sons. How could one's blessing pass to two people? It didn't. Remember, the tribe of Levi got no land. They were the law-keepers, the religious staff.

Numbers 1 records the removal of Levi. He didn't have any land, and the swapping of Joseph with his sons pulled two original tribe names out and inserted Joseph's sons.

Numbers 26 records Reuben to Asher correctly and then Manasseh/Joseph and Ephraim, and leaves out Levi. That was because Levi was scattered throughout the tribes and counted with the tribe they were closest to.

For the sons of Joseph were two tribes, Manasseh and Ephraim, and they did not give a portion to the Levites in the land, except cities to live in, with their pasture lands for their livestock and for their property. Thus the sons of Israel did just as the Lord had commanded Moses, and they divided the land."

—Josh. 14:4–5

There is one list that has confused many people, and I want to dwell on that for a second.

And I heard the number of those who were sealed, one hundred and forty-four thousand sealed from every tribe of the sons of Israel:

from the tribe of Judah, twelve thousand were sealed, from the tribe of Reuben twelve thousand, from the tribe of Gad twelve thousand, from the tribe of Asher twelve thousand, from the tribe of Naphtali twelve thousand, from the tribe of Manasseh twelve thousand, from the tribe of Simeon twelve thousand, from the tribe of Levi twelve thousand, from the tribe of Issachar twelve thousand, from the tribe of Zebulun twelve thousand, from the tribe of Joseph twelve thousand, from the tribe of Benjamin, twelve thousand were sealed.

—Rev. 7:4–8

	Original			Revelation
1	Reuben		1	Judah
2	Simeon		2	Reuben
3	Levi		3	Gad
4	Judah		4	Asher
5	Zebulun		5	Naphtali
6	Issachar		6	Manasseh
7	Dan		7	Simeon
8	Gad		8	Levi
9	Asher		9	Issachar
10	Naphtali		10	Zebulun
11	Joseph		11	Joseph
12	Benjamin		12	Benjamin

Notice the difference. In Genesis, Dan was included, but not in Revelation. This is simple if my opinion of who the 144,000 are is true. Herod tried to kill Jesus when he was a baby, but then Dan didn't lose any babies during this massacre. Thus his tribe didn't have any "firstfruits" of Christ. It's simple. I cover this pretty thoroughly in *Enough Chaos Volume 1*.

And if you are wondering why Manasseh is there but not Ephraim, that is simple too. Look back at Numbers 25. They threw Joseph in with Manasseh. This time, they threw him in with Ephraim. No biggie. When the dad is there, he gets his name on the list first.

Now . . . *why does this matter to Christians?*

Part of the answer is below.

Then Peter said to Him, "Behold, we have left everything and followed You; what then will there be for us?" And Jesus said to them, "Truly I say to you, that you who have followed Me, in the regeneration when the Son of Man will sit on His glorious throne, you also shall sit upon twelve thrones, judging the twelve tribes of Israel. And everyone who has left houses or brothers or sisters or father or mother or children or farms for My name's sake, will receive many times as much, and will inherit eternal life. But many who are first will be last; and the last, first.

—Matt. 19:27–30

If you want to see what this will look like, look at Revelation 21—all of it.

The other part, the part I need ya'll to understand, is in the next chapter of this book.

MELCHIZEDEK

Why is this important?

This is critical to understand when forming an opinion of our relationship to the modern-day Jewish religion. There is a passage in the New Testament that threw me for a roller-coaster-sized loop when I first read it.

For this Melchizedek, king of Salem, priest of the Most High God, who met Abraham as he was returning from the slaughter of the kings and blessed him, to whom also Abraham apportioned a tenth part of all the spoils, was first of all, by the translation of his name, king of righteousness, and then also king of Salem, which is king of peace. Without father, without mother, without genealogy, having neither beginning of days nor end of life, but made like the Son of God, he remains a priest perpetually.

Now observe how great this man was to whom Abraham, the patriarch, gave a tenth of the choicest spoils. And those indeed of the sons of Levi who receive the priest's office have commandment in the Law to collect a tenth from the people, that is, from their brethren, although these are descended from Abraham. But the one whose genealogy is not traced from them collected a tenth from Abraham and blessed the one who had the promises.

—Heb. 7:1–6

In this case, mortal men receive tithes, but in that case, one receives them, of whom it is witnessed that he lives on. And, so to speak, through Abraham even Levi, who received tithes, paid tithes.

—Heb. 7:8–9

Now if perfection was through the Levitical priesthood (for on the basis of it the people received the Law), what further need was there for another priest to arise according to the order of Melchizedek, and not be designated according to the order of Aaron? For when the priesthood is changed, of necessity there takes place a change of law also. For the one concerning whom these things are spoken belongs to another tribe, from which no one has officiated at the altar. For it is evident that our Lord was descended from Judah, a tribe with reference to which Moses spoke nothing concerning priests. And this is clearer still, if another priest arises according to the likeness of Melchizedek, who has become such not on the basis of a law of physical requirement, but according to the power of an indestructible life. For it is attested of Him,

"You are a priest forever
According to the order of Melchizedek."

For, on the one hand, there is a setting aside of a former commandment because of its weakness and uselessness (for the Law made nothing perfect), and on the other hand there is a bringing in of a better hope, through which we draw near to God. And inasmuch as it was not without an oath (for they indeed became priests without an oath, but He with an oath through the One who said to Him,

*"The Lord has sworn
And will not change His mind,
'You are a priest forever'");
so much the more also Jesus has become the guarantee of a better covenant.*

The former priests, on the one hand, existed in greater numbers because they were prevented by death from continuing, but Jesus, on the other hand, because He continues forever, holds His priesthood permanently. Therefore He is able also to save forever those who draw near to God through Him, since He always lives to make intercession for them.

For it was fitting for us to have such a high priest, holy, innocent, undefiled, separated from sinners and exalted above the heavens; who does not need daily, like those high priests, to offer up sacrifices, first for His own sins and then for the sins of the people, because this He did once for all when He offered up Himself. For the Law appoints men as high priests who are weak, but the word of the oath, which came after the Law, appoints **a** *Son, made perfect forever.*

—Heb. 7:11–28

I read this passage and thought, *What?*

Christ was a priest on earth in the New Testament.

Hebrews 7:3 says Melchizedek had no mom and no dad. Or was this another immaculate being without being born? Was this an angel?

What?

Like most times, the veil was lifted from my eyes by another brother, a man I consider my elder, regardless of his station in the church.

Here is a *very rough* breakdown of Hebrews 7.

Christ is better than your Jewish priests.

A long time ago, your forefather (Abraham) went to battle trying to save Lot. He brought back spoils of war and gave 10 percent to Melchizedek, the high priest of that area. Abraham paid a tithe to this other guy.

Jesus is both high priest and king, just like Melchizedek was. You (Jews) track who can be a priest by their father and mother, and thus they are of the tribe of Levi. Christ, being under the order of Melchizedek, doesn't care what tribe you are from because Abraham was *under* the domain of Melchizedek.

Then after his return from the defeat of Chedorlaomer and the kings who were with him, the king of Sodom went out to meet him at the valley of Shaveh (that is, the King's Valley). And Melchizedek king of Salem brought out bread and wine; now he was a priest of God Most High. He blessed him and said,

"Blessed be Abram of God Most High,
Possessor of heaven and earth;
And blessed be God Most High,
Who has delivered your enemies into your hand."

161

He gave him a tenth of all. The king of Sodom said to Abram, "Give the people to me and take the goods for yourself." Abram said to the king of Sodom, "I have sworn to the Lord God Most High, possessor of heaven and earth, that I will not take a thread or a sandal thong or anything that is yours, for fear you would say, 'I have made Abram rich.' I will take nothing except what the young men have eaten, and the share of the men who went with me, Aner, Eshcol, and Mamre; let them take their share."

—Gen. 14:17–24

The Lord says to my Lord:
"Sit at My right hand
Until I make Your enemies a footstool for Your feet."
The LORD will stretch forth Your strong scepter from Zion, saying,
"Rule in the midst of Your enemies."
Your people will volunteer freely in the day of Your power;
In holy array, from the womb of the dawn,
Your youth are to You as the dew.
The Lord has sworn and will not change His mind,
"You are a priest forever
According to the order of Melchizedek."

—Ps. 110:1–4

I have heard many men tell me that they do their best to read their Bible, but in the end, they just try to be nice, obey the 10 commandments, and always tithe their 10 percent.

This makes the Holy Spirit within me almost *Roar* with frustration.

When you embrace the laws of the Old Testament and ignore the direction of the New Testament, you throw Christ's sacrifice out too. In all honesty, you are following a lesser code of ethics, a less superior and a less perfect covenant for Gentiles.

Usually, men say this to me, but what I believe they are saying in their mind is this: "I am too lazy to sit down and figure out the New Testament, so I found a list somewhere, and I think that is good enough."

God does not agree with you in this matter, I promise. God made a covenant with Abraham a long time ago, and he gave him rules to follow. God even said he would preserve the remnants of Abraham's seed, and he has done that. They refused to follow him and were destroyed down to a single tribe we call the Jewish religion today. They refused to adhere to his Word.

We as Christians might want to start listening to everything he has said and start living like we are supposed to, both in mind and in action. The 12 tribes are our cousins, and they are a mission-critical lesson for us as followers of Christ under the Order of Melchizedek. Christ is my high priest. Christ is my king.

P.S. The word *Salem* means peace. He is the *king of peace*. The old, old Melchizedek was the king of the city of Salem as a foreshadowing of Christ being the king of peace.

Go back and look at the 12 tribes in Genesis 49:10. This is referencing when Shiloh comes. This is the millennial reign of Christ.

This is my king.

DO PETS GO TO HEAVEN?

Why is this important?

Do you like believing lies?

Does the Bible support your believing and propagating lies?

First, let's see the wording in the Bible for both the creating of animals and the creation of man.

Then God said, "Let the earth bring forth living creatures after their kind: cattle and creeping things and beasts of the earth after their kind"; and it was so. God made the beasts of the earth after their kind, and the cattle after their kind, and everything that creeps on the ground after its kind; and God saw that it was good.

—Gen. 1:24–25

Then God said, "Let Us make man in Our image, according to Our likeness; and let them rule over the fish of the sea and over the birds of the sky and over the cattle and over all the earth, and over every creeping thing that creeps on the earth." God created man in His own image, in the image of God He created him; male and female He created them.

—Gen. 1:26–27

Then the LORD God formed man of dust from the ground, and breathed into his nostrils the breath of life; and man became a living being.

—Gen. 2:7

Now let's see if anyone in the Bible made a clear distinction between animal life and human life.

But now ask the beasts, and let them teach you;
And the birds of the heavens, and let them tell you.
Or speak to the earth, and let it teach you;
And let the fish of the sea declare to you.
Who among all these does not know
That the hand of the Lord has done this,
In whose hand is the life of every living thing,
And the breath of all mankind?

—Job 12:7–10

"Life of every living thing, and the breath of all mankind"—it looks like Job saw a difference between man and animal.

Here is a verse some use to imply that animals go to heaven.

And every created thing which is in heaven and on the earth and under the earth and on the sea, and all things in them, I heard saying,

"To Him who sits on the throne, and to the Lamb, be blessing and honor and glory and dominion forever and ever."

—Rev. 5:13

There are two ways to counter the idea that pets die and go to heaven when this verse is used to support it.

Option A: There are multiple heavens. This is fact according to the Bible.

Then God said, "Let there be an expanse in the midst of the waters, and let it separate the waters from the waters." God made the expanse, and separated the waters which were below the expanse from the waters which were above the expanse; and it was so. God called the expanse heaven. And there was evening and there was morning, a second day.

—Gen. 1:6–8

The first heaven is the place where the birds fly and the football soars through the air to the receiver's hands. It is the air we breathe. It is what we call the atmosphere.

Our dead giveaway that this reference could be talking about the first heaven is the statements from Revelation 5.

Heaven = ?
Earth = land animals
Under the earth = cave animals, dirt crawlers
Sea = water animals

What kind of animal is missing from this equation?

Or you could also try to say that "under the earth" means things in hell, but again, look at the context of the statement.

What makes more sense?

Earth = land animals
Under the earth = cave animals, dirt crawlers
Sea = water animals

Or

Earth = land animals
Under the earth = things in hell (?)
Sea = water animals

It is clear to me that the author is talking about animals living in caves as well as below the ground like worms (in this example).

So if the below is correct . . .

Heaven =
Earth = land animals
Under the earth = cave animals, dirt crawlers
Sea = water animals

Then what animals are missing from the equation? That's right, birds. Birds fly in the first heaven.

With this, Option A is squashed.

Option B is that this verse is describing every single thing God created that has some form of life, whether only in spirit form or as a fully operational body to move around in.

If this is the case, then the list would look like the one below.

Heaven = angelic hosts
Earth = land animals, humans on earth
Under the earth = dead asleep, people in hell pre-flood
Sea = water animals, people on boats

To use this paintbrush is so wide that it cannot logically be used to imply that creatures mean pets in heaven.

The dead giveaway that this statement is referring to all three heavens at once is when we read Revelation 5:13 and 14 back to back.

And every created thing which is in heaven and on the earth and under the earth and on the sea, and all things in them, I heard saying,

"To Him who sits on the throne, and to the Lamb, be blessing and honor and glory and dominion forever and ever."

And the four living creatures kept saying, "Amen." And the elders fell down and worshiped.

—Rev. 5:13–14

And when we understand the entirety of Revelation 5, we understand that this is the proving process before Christ opens the seals. It is where everything in creation is being asked who is worthy enough to take the seals.

And I saw a strong angel proclaiming with a loud voice, "Who is worthy to open the book and to break its seals?"

—Rev. 5:2

Christ steps up and takes the seal, and "every created thing" agrees that Christ is worthy.

Some other prop-up verses are in Ecclesiastes 3.

I said to myself concerning the sons of men, "God has surely tested them in order for them to see that they are but beasts." For the fate of the sons of men and the fate of beasts is the same. As one dies so dies the other; indeed, they all have the same breath and there is no advantage for man over beast, for all is vanity. All go to the same place. All came from the dust and all return to the dust. Who knows that the breath of man ascends upward and the breath of the beast descends downward to the earth?

—Eccles. 3:18–21

Solomon, the Old Testament author, is talking about their flesh going into the soil, but in the next verse, he is wondering. This is his private thought written down. This is his journal. He is actively wondering, "Who knows?"

I think it is folly to try to prop up your idea that pets go to heaven based on a Bible verse where someone is asking a question in their private journal, don't you?

Another series of prop-up verses are the references to horses coming down from heaven.

I looked, and behold, a white horse, and the one who sat on it had a bow; and a crown was given to him, and he went out conquering and to conquer. . . . And another, a red horse, went out; and to him who sat on it, it was granted to take peace from the earth, and that men would slay one another; and a large sword was given to him.

—Rev. 6:2, 4

When He broke the third seal, I heard the third living creature saying, "Come!" I looked, and behold, a black horse, and he who sat on it had a pair of scales in his hand.

—Rev. 6:5

I looked, and behold, an ashen horse; and he who sat on it had the name Death, and Hades was following with him. Authority was given to them over a fourth of the earth, to kill with sword and famine and with pestilence and by the wild beasts of the earth.

—Rev. 6:8

And I saw heaven opened, and behold, a white horse, and He who sat on it is called Faithful and True, and in righteousness He judges and wages war.

—Rev. 19:11

And the armies which are in heaven, clothed in fine linen, white and clean, were following Him on white horses.

—Rev. 19:14

But we clearly have a previous chapter where Christ rode on an angel.

And He rode on a cherub and flew;
And He appeared on the wings of the wind.

—2 Sam. 22:11

In my opinion, when John says in Revelation that he saw a horse, that was the vision he was shown.

Think of it like this. In Revelations 12, John sees a woman in the sky.

*A great sign appeared in heaven: a woman clothed with
the sun, and the moon under her feet, and on her head a
crown of twelve stars.*

—Rev. 12:1

This is a metaphor for Israel, *but* it is also the constellation
Virgo (more about this in another chapter). For this one
moment, please believe me. John saw a vision that was a
double metaphor. We are not all to be looking for a real-life
floating woman. He saw the constellation, Virgo.

John the Revelator often saw in metaphors.

David on the other hand physically saw an event in real-
time.

My opinion is that when these "horses" are mentioned,
they will be a version of angels that are being ridden.

Sorry, cowboys and cowgirls. When Rocket and Root Beer
die, they die.

The big slayer of this theory is when we look at how God
treats animals.

*And the LORD God made for Adam and for his wife
garments of skins and clothed them.*

—Gen. 3:21 ESV

So it looks like God killed an animal to make clothing for
Adam and Eve. Could he have remade just the animal skins?
Sure, but what is an easier jump?

A to B?

Or A to B to C? You are adding an extra thing.

My opinion is that it was a simple act of killing, skinning, and shaping, which we as humans do all the time. That is *modifying* a previous creation.

If God had created something entirely new such as an animal skin that was just "poofed" into existence, that would have been a *new creation*. But he created everything in six days, right?

And it wouldn't have taught Adam and Eve anything. Killing an animal and fashioning clothes let them see how to clothe themselves properly. I have no proof that he did the skinning and sewing in front of Adam and Eve, but I wouldn't be surprised.

If you are not convinced of this, wait until you see what happens in Noah's time.

> *And all flesh died that moved on the earth, birds, livestock, beasts, all swarming creatures that swarm on the earth, and all mankind.*
>
> —Gen. 7:21 ESV

God kills everything on land because of the original sin of Adam. Do you still think animals and humans are the same? But wait. It gets worse.

> *The fear of you and the dread of you shall be upon every beast of the earth and upon every bird of the heavens, upon everything that creeps on the ground and all the fish of the sea. Into your hand they are delivered. Every moving thing that lives shall be food for you. And as I gave you the green plants, I give you everything.*
>
> —Gen. 9:2–3 ESV

Holy moly superstars! Did you guys just see where God gave us permission to eat animals? Granted, there were some rules given to Noah and then later to the 12 tribes, but this is an undeniable point. These creatures are to be food for us.

Whoever sheds the blood of man,
by man shall his blood be shed,
for God made man in his own image.

—Gen. 9:6 ESV

God makes it abundantly clear that humans are not to be killed. There is a clear and obvious difference between humans and animals.

And he said to them, "Go." So they came out and went into the pigs, and behold, the whole herd rushed down the steep bank into the sea and drowned in the waters.

—Matt. 8:32 ESV

Whoa, boy! Christ sends and allows demons to go into a pig. Regardless of what is a clean creature or not, this is a pig created by the Creator. What did it do to deserve this? Nothing. But it is an animal, and there is a clear difference between how God treats mankind and animals.

Look at the birds of the air: they neither sow nor reap nor gather into barns, and yet your heavenly Father feeds them. Are you not of more value than they?

—Matt. 6:26 ESV

Christ even makes a very clear difference between how God takes care of animals and how much more will he take care of you because ... because ... come on, people ... because we are more important.

I don't care what your personal feelings are about this subject. If you are a Christian, you are called to reject lies.

Jesus answered him, "Truly, truly, I say to you, unless one is born again he cannot see the kingdom of God."

—John 3:3 ESV

So there are no back doors into heaven, at least for people. And doesn't God care more for people than animals? If anyone was going to get a back door into heaven, shouldn't it be us?

For all have sinned and fall short of the glory of God.

—Rom. 3:23 ESV

Everybody has sinned, right?

No, I tell you; but unless you repent, you will all likewise perish.

—Luke 13:3 ESV

Can a dog repent of its sins?

Because, if you confess with your mouth that Jesus is Lord and believe in your heart that God raised him from the dead, you will be saved.

—Rom. 10: 9 ESV

Does your pet fish confess with its mouth that Jesus is Lord?

If you love me, you will keep my commandments.

—John 14:15 ESV

Does your pet ferret keep God's commandments?

Whoever believes and is baptized will be saved, but whoever does not believe will be condemned.

—Mark 16:16 ESV

Does your pet parrot believe in Christ, and has it been baptized? If not, sorry.

Animals can demonstrate many emotions, but the big hitch, the point killer, the last shot, the big burrito is this:

can they recognize their wrongs and repent? I don't mean a dog covering his poop. After all, he is scared of his owner's reaction, because he has been taught that this is bad. I am not talking about conditioning habits such as potty training. Crows can be trained too.

I am talking about recognizing their wrongs, repenting directly to God, and attempting to make amends.

Let's look at some of the more extreme animal behaviors, and let me ask you a single question.

Do you think the animals discussed below feel shame?

Male dogs will often attempt to rape anything in sight, from other dogs to stuffed animals to your leg. This is called attempted rape, and if you were not as big as you are . . .

Many of them often eat poop too.

Many animals are what science has labeled "surplus killers." I call it killing for fun. They include honey badgers, bears, dogs, orcas, and cats.

House cats have been recorded eating the body parts of their owner after they die.

Dogs have been recorded actually killing their owner and then eating their body parts.

When female ferrets go into heat, they either *must* have intercourse or they could potentially die. Male ferrets commit what can only be described as domestic violence as a form of getting the female's body to be "ready."

Rhinos are often sexually assaulted by elephants (This is arguable).

Penguins are often sexually assaulted by seals.

Dead penguins are often sexually assaulted by penguins.

Penguin chicks are often sexually assaulted by penguins.

Penguin mothers have been recorded stealing babies from other penguins to raise them as their own.

Zebras will assault a pregnant female, cause a miscarriage, and then mate with her.

Dolphin males have been recorded as teaming up, stealing a female from a different pod (family), and then sexually assaulting her repeatedly for up to a month.

If panda mothers have two kids, they will sometimes pick their favorite and abandon the other, regardless of predators and food sources.

The bottlenose dolphin has been seen using its boy part to grab an electric eel and provide "release."

A mother quokka, also known as the short-tailed scrub wallaby, will discard her babies if a predator is chasing them. It's creating a distraction so she can get away. Kangaroos do that too.

There are a ton of species where the mother eats her children for one reason or another. Birds, rodents, rabbits, fish, frogs—they all do it.

There are a lot of species where the male kills all the kids in a pack or nest before mating with the females. Bears, lions, chimps—they all do it.

There are a bunch of species where the firstborn immediately eats all the other babies and eggs. Snails, sharks, birds, frogs—they all do it.

Blacklace spider mothers are devoured by their babies.

Female Australian redback spiders will eat a part of the male during intercourse. If he survives, he comes back for round two and usually does not survive. The black widow and praying mantis version of this are only when food is scarce.

You may see the natural world just being "natural." I see a world covered in sin because of what Adam did.

My little children, I am writing these things to you so that you may not sin. But if anyone does sin, we have an advocate with the Father, Jesus Christ the righteous. He is the propitiation for our sins, and not for ours only but also for the sins of the whole world. And by this we know that we have come to know him, if we keep his commandments.

—1 John 2:1–3 ESV

Humans have committed versions of all the above, but they also can accept redemption, be redeemed, and go forward and sin no more.

Does anyone think any of the animals felt guilt after they committed the above acts?

Do you think the seal sat back a day later and regretted sexually assaulting the penguin?

Do you really think your dog regrets pooping on the rug? Do you think he genuinely regrets it? No, he regrets getting caught and your coming up with a newspaper and swatting him . . . or hippie browbeating him . . . or verbally discouraging him, which is training him to fear negative reinforcement. Training and genuine guilt are two different things.

There was a study done once about a mouse (I believe). Mouse A was fed, and Mouse B got shocked, inflicted with pain. Mouse A stopped eating and went into starvation rather than intentionally inflict pain on Mouse B. I would *love* to reference this experiment, but I can't because I can't remember where I heard it. I researched while I was writing this book and found several similar research reports altering things here and there. They all came to the same conclusion.

I believe there was even a study that showed that a non-natural fear—something they wouldn't come into contact with in the wild—can be created and *genetically* passed on to its offspring *without the offspring ever coming into contact with it.*

Let that sink in.

A mouse gets hurt every time it "chews on bubblegum." It learns and avoids bubblegum. The researchers pull that mouse and let it have children. They take those children and let them become adults. Then they move them to another tank and *walla!* This mouse avoids bubblegum too.

This has been repeated a couple of times in a few ways, but overall, they got the same result.

I *love* science and figuring out what God has done, created, and will do. Shout out to everyone who has taken part in these studies. There are too many of ya'll to list.

But the presence of emotions is *not* the separation between humans and animals. Neither is memory or thought or problem-solving. On their own, they do not have a natural limiter switch for what is right and what is wrong. We do. Many cultures in the past have tried to beat it down and subdue that limiter switch (e.g., slavery, torture, murder, rape), but the switch was always there inside the person being stifled. We teach our children to cover the switch in varying degrees.

When a human has completely killed this limiter switch, they can be diagnosed as a sociopath or even a psychopath.

Serial rape in a human would make a psychopath, but in a seal, it is just called being an animal that is covered in sin. They don't go to heaven, but they don't go to hell either.

God spoke in the days of Noah about this limiter switch being covered.

And when the Lord smelled the pleasing aroma, the Lord said in his heart, "I will never again curse the ground because of man, for the intention of man's heart is evil from his youth. Neither will I ever again strike down every living creature as I have done.

—Gen. 8:21 ESV

We, humans, are the only creatures who can receive salvation and thus get into heaven-heaven. That's not the atmosphere; it's way, way, way up there—heaven.

Here is another set of verses people use to prop up this theory.

For not all flesh is the same, but there is one kind for humans, another for animals, another for birds, and another for fish. There are heavenly bodies and earthly bodies, but the glory of the heavenly is of one kind, and the glory of the earthly is of another. There is one glory of the sun, and another glory of the moon, and another glory of the stars; for star differs from star in glory. So is it with the resurrection of the dead. What is sown is perishable; what is raised is imperishable.

—1 Cor. 15:39–42 ESV

I cannot fathom how this points to the idea that animals will be resurrected in heaven. This is the author showing how different things are and then saying that "our future body" will be that different from our "current body."

Keep reading. It gets even clearer.

It is sown in dishonor, it is raised in glory. It is sown in weakness, it is raised in power.

—1 Cor. 15:43 ESV

It's old life and then new life.

It is sown a natural body; it is raised a spiritual body. If there is a natural body, there is also a spiritual body.

—1 Cor. 15:44 ESV

Here is a single statement that could be used to prop it up, but the next verse makes it clear *exactly* who we are talking about.

Thus it is written, "The first man Adam became a living being"; the last Adam became a life-giving spirit. But it is not the spiritual that is first but the natural, and then the spiritual. The first man was from the earth, a man of dust; the second man is from heaven.

—1 Cor. 15:45–47 ESV

Isaiah 11 is talking about animals in general, not your redeemed pets.

The wolf shall dwell with the lamb,
and the leopard shall lie down with the young goat,
and the calf and the lion and the fattened calf together;
and a little child shall lead them.
The cow and the bear shall graze;
their young shall lie down together;
and the lion shall eat straw like the ox.

—Isa. 11:6–7 ESV

This is made clear if we keep reading.

They shall not hurt or destroy
in all my holy mountain;
for the earth shall be full of the knowledge of the Lord
as the waters cover the sea.

—Isa. 11:9 ESV

There is a ton of references to "redeeming all flesh" and "creation being liberated from sin," and yes, these would include the animals . . . *on earth.* The earth will be atoned for. It is called the Feast of Atonement. Then we have the Isaiah

9 situation, which is what the Feast of Tabernacles points to—Christ's millennial reign, peace, and hippie happiness for everyone.

Learn your feasts of the Lord; it makes things like this easier to understand. It's kind of cool how God gave Christians the feasts so we could understand what was going to happen. You might want to start learning about them.

PERSONALITY TESTS

(Enneagram, Love Languages, Meyers Briggs, Flag Page)

I am going to be honest with you, family. I am pulled on this chapter. There are two very real and very different views on personality tests. There is a third view, and I will call that one the old man view. I refer to it as such because it was an old man who first shared it with me. That is the easiest one to capture, so let's start there.

Opinion 1 – Old Man View: I don't need nothin' but the Bible. Everything else just detracts from worshiping and focusing on God.

Biblical Backing:

> *If any of you lacks wisdom, let him ask God, who gives generously to all without reproach, and it will be given him.*
>
> —James 1:5 ESV

Old Man Thought:

The Bible doesn't tell me to fill out a test to get to know myself. The Lord knows me, and I will ask him.

My Rebuttal:

Do you ask the Lord to give you information to give to your doctor during your yearly physical? Or do you let the doctor do a blood draw and send it off to the lab for analysis by a machine?

Do you ask the Lord to give you information to give to your car mechanic? Or do you let them hook up their diagnostic machine to your car's computer so they can narrow down the problems?

Do you build your own virus software and clean your own computer, or do you let the expert geek do expert geek things?

Did you refuse to fill out the ASVAB before getting into the military? Do you know that the ASVAB is a placement exam(ish)?

Did you refuse to fill out the SATs, which is a college placement exam?

Did you refuse to let your child take STAR testing, which is a test designed to weigh a child's academic prowess against where experts believe they should be at that age?

Did you refuse to perform the chlorine test for your pool?

See how silly things can get when someone refuses to take a non-invasive test because God will provide the information?

In fact, you could go hyper-crazy and imply that our eyes and ears are versions of computers that process data. How much better followers of Christ could be if we deafened and blinded ourselves and relied solely on the Lord to provide the information to our brains for our daily lives.

I have no problem with you as a person deciding for yourself to abstain from a personality test, but people like that always tend to put other people down for their desire to take them.

If you want to know more about everything, of course, you

can and should ask God, but please remember, God has also allowed us to make some tools for these purposes.

Are we going to deny medication to a person because God is the ultimate healer?

or

Do we treat the injury as best we know how and pray for healing? It will be God's will, but we will try our best to treat the patient.

My family, this is a murky matter, and it may seem a cut-and-dried, yes-or-no kind of issue, but it is a question that carries some very real and very tangible results if we start pulling this string.

Old Man View Summation:

Saying no just to say no is stupid. Have a real opinion, a real reason, rightly dividing the Word of truth. If you don't want to do it, just say I don't want to do it, dad-gum grumpy old men.

Now that I have demonstrated how flip-floppy and confusing this can be, we can look at Opinions 2 and 3.

Opinion 2: Personality tests are wonderful and should always be embraced. They can only do good things for you. How can finding out more about yourself be wrong?

Opinion 3: Personality tests with roots in the occult should be avoided, but the rest are okay or at least less anti-biblical.

And finally, here is my view.

Opinion 4 – *Enough Chaos* view: It's all or nothing as long as everything stays below the Bible and every tool is in its proper place. Discernment is key.

To start off with a bang, I am going to lift up some ladies with occult experience before coming to Christianity.

On YouTube, Alisa Childers and Marcia Montenegro have a fantastic conversation about the Enneagram test, its roots, its origins, and the potential effects it could unintentionally have on our culture. I ask you to watch that (if the channel and platform are still up when you are reading this).

YouTube Channel	Alisa Childers
Video Title	"From the Occult to the Church: How Enneagram Became Part of Christian Culture"
Publication Date	January 5, 2021
Web Link	https://www.youtube.com/watch?v=1J2G0k_PaYM

Another fantastic lady, Melissa Dougherty, did a great review.

YouTube Channel	Melissa Dougherty
Video Title	"The #1 Reason I Believe the Enneagram Is Deceptive"
Publication Date	March 15, 2021
Web Link	https://www.youtube.com/watch?v=cYKlUR-3Vxo

As a Christian with the mind of a statistician, I have a very peculiar perspective, and I love a good challenge. For this reason, I will do my best to represent both sides of the equation to their truest height. And then I will bring in my view.

Considering how very lazy most of us are and also engaging the possibility that you may not have access to a computer—and maybe YouTube is not a thing when you are reading this—I will give you the Cliff Notes of both of these videos.

I beg you to stop and go watch these ladies' works. They are intelligent and informative, even if you don't agree with everything they say. I have not done deep dives on *either* of these ladies' theology, so I am not lifting them up for that reason. I'm just focusing on these two works. Also, I deliberately chose females because the New Age movement is largely popular with females, so I wanted a genuine female perspective.

P.S. Below are my personal notes on their videos, so please forgive the scatterbrained nature of the notes.

Alisa Childers and Marcia Montenegro on the Enneagram
Origin: 1916. Define Enneagram. Enneagram is "key to everything." It has nothing to do with personalities at first. In the '60s, the spiritual aspect started getting taught. It deeply describes the relationship to false self and ego. *Smart lady.* Came to California, drugs, got introduced to the equation in the '70s. Auto writing based on spirit contact. Lots of references to "big" people who caught the Enneagram movement. In 2016 it goes mainstream with a "Christian" book release. She really, really is a *smart lady.*

Melissa Dougherty
Defined Enneagram, a New Age sacred tool as a path to enlightenment or embracing your inner god. People do it because they are bored. Need cultural fulfillment. Marcia Montenegro highlight. Origin, the late 1800s. Richard Rohr

highlights, "finding purpose within yourself and not the Bible." Spirits origin. Excellent point: you will judge people by this and not by who they are. She doesn't point-blank say this, but the point is clear. Lifts up the book *Richard Rohr and the Enneagram Secret*.

So overall, this point of view is that the Enneagram is from demonic sources, was originally part of the New Age movement, and was then "smuggled" into Christianity. It runs a risk of both taking the focus off of God, the Bible, and the Holy Spirit and leaning on the devil and the works of demons to somehow advance ourselves.

Look at Opinion 2: "Personality tests are wonderful and should always be embraced. They can only do good things for you. How can finding out more about yourself be wrong?"

It kind of loses that lackluster appeal, huh?

Anyone who has or does believe in the Enneagram probably has a little awkward—oops—head-scratching thing going on right now. I know.

My Enneagram is a Type 7 with a Wing 8, meaning I am an enthusiast who leans heavily on the challenger mindset. But according to the teachings, if I want to be more "balanced," I need to work on my Type 6, which is loyalty. Okay.

I took this thing a long time ago during my first divorce. It was recommended to me by my marriage therapist as a possible tool to help me and my wife relate better. We got a divorce, so . . . no.

Let me ask you all something. Reading this book so far, does anyone see me as an enthusiast? Or do you all see me more as a challenger? Yeah, exactly.

Here is Opinion 4: *Enough Chaos* view: It's all or nothing as long as everything stays below the Bible and every tool is in its proper place. Discernment is key.

The Enneagram cannot be used by Christians because it comes from spirits. Period. It cannot ever be below the Bible because it is against the Bible.

Beloved, do not believe every spirit, but test the spirits to see whether they are from God, for many false prophets have gone out into the world.

—1 John 4:1 ESV

Did the founding person of this idea "test" the spirits before receiving these auto-writings, spirit-led revelations?

For we do not wrestle against flesh and blood, but against the rulers, against the authorities, against the cosmic powers over this present darkness, against the spiritual forces of evil in the heavenly places.

—Eph. 6:12 ESV

Do not turn to mediums or necromancers; do not seek them out, and so make yourselves unclean by them: I am the Lord your God.

—Lev. 19:31 ESV

Behold, I and the children whom the Lord has given me are signs and portents in Israel from the Lord of hosts, who dwells on Mount Zion. And when they say to you, "Inquire of the mediums and the necromancers who chirp and mutter," should not a people inquire of their God? Should they inquire of the dead on behalf of the living?

—Isa. 8:18–19 ESV

So we are called to test all spirits, but more on that later.

In *Enough Chaos, Volume 1*, I slammed Christians for using the book of Leviticus to preach against homosexuality because it is cherry-picking Scripture. Remember Opinion 4, all or nothing? This is my belief, and I beg of you to please let me dazzle you.

Here is my biblical shout-out for this chapter too.

An accuser could take my "leaning on Leviticus" and say, "Oh yeah, well Leviticus 19:27 says not to cut your beards. Do you obey that too?" And If I leaned back on Leviticus as most Christians do, I would be a hypocrite by my own mouth.

My response to that person would be, "You're right, sir/ma'am."

And the LORD spoke to Moses, saying, "Speak to all the congregation of the people of Israel and say to them, You shall be holy, for I the Lord your God am holy.

—Lev. 19:1–2 ESV

Clearly, these are God's instructions to his children, the 12 tribes, the second invited to the feast. Not to me. I am a Gentile, the bastard brought in from the street to be the third invited to the feast.

You shall not round off the hair on your temples or mar the edges of your beard.

—Lev. 19:27 ESV

I am a gentile. I can cut my beard all I want because I have a different set of rules. A better set of rules. Let me show you my rules, the New Testament of my Lord and Savior Jesus Christ.

*Beware of false prophets, who come to you in sheep's
clothing but inwardly are ravenous wolves. You will
recognize them by their fruits. Are grapes gathered from
thornbushes, or figs from thistles? So, every healthy tree
bears good fruit, but the diseased tree bears bad fruit. A
healthy tree cannot bear bad fruit, nor can a diseased
tree bear good fruit. Every tree that does not bear good
fruit is cut down and thrown into the fire. Thus you will
recognize them by their fruits.*

—Matt. 7:15–20 ESV

God told me in 1 John 4 to test all spirits. My Christian
sisters have presented evidence that the Enneagram came
from communicating with spirits. I cannot confirm that the
originator did test the spirits, nor can I even confirm that the
author was a Christian.

If it was from God, it would be considered new scripture.

That is not the biggest hiccup in the logic of calling this
scripture.

The biggest hiccup is that it looks *nothing* like anything
Christ has ever said to anyone in the Bible.

So it came from an *unknown source* and looks nothing like
Christ's previous words.

Here is where I boil down all the arguments.

What can you lose if you throw this "tool" away? Nothing
other than this seemingly harmless tool, right?

What can you lose if you embrace this tool? You have
no clue because you cannot see all the spiderwebs of the
darkness. Just like we were tricked in the Garden of Eden
with Satan's fancy words, we could also be misled by this
fancy trick.

It tastes good, but it sours the stomach.

As a statistician, it is all about numbers. What am I risking by throwing this test out? What am I risking by embracing this test?

We have sisters who have done a lot of research into its origins. You might want to give it a listen before you make the wrong decision.

This, my family, is what teaching discernment and leaning on fellow Christians looks like versus teaching pulpit obedience.

P.S. Thank you, ladies, for all your hard work. If you, the reader, agree, you might want to let them know on their YouTube platforms.

Hey! Ya'll remember the Old Man View? It's funny how we got to the same place but with a critical difference. The Old Man View says no but doesn't know why he says no. The *Enough Chaos* View says no because it is not worth being wrong. My sisters have evidence, and it sounds nothing like Christ.

We don't say no just to say no. We rightly divide the Word of God. If we are unsure, we take it to our deacons or pastors for shepherding. We share our findings with the rest of the body (like distributing antibodies throughout the body) so other Christians don't fall into our potholes, *and* in case our pastors are wrong, we can see that too.

If your church is embracing Enneagram, feel free to take a copy of this book to your pastor and ask him to read this section. Then ask him to explain how much research he has conducted into the origins of the Enneagram.

When he says it was recommended by a friend or he

saw another church doing it, please ask the question again because clearly, the pastor didn't understand the question.

Feel free to show him the verses below.

Not many of you should become teachers, my brothers, for you know that we who teach will be judged with greater strictness.

—James 3:1 ESV

But whoever causes one of these little ones who believe in me to sin, it would be better for him to have a great millstone fastened around his neck and to be drowned in the depth of the sea.

—Matt. 18:6 ESV

She said, "No one, Lord." And Jesus said, "Neither do I condemn you; go, and from now on sin no more."

—John 8:11 ESV

It is up to you whether to apply the verses below.

Do not admit a charge against an elder except on the evidence of two or three witnesses. As for those who persist in sin, rebuke them in the presence of all, so that the rest may stand in fear.

—1 Tim. 5:19–20 ESV

Next on the Chopping Block: Love Languages

Right out of the gate, good ol' Glen is this when it comes to love languages:

Physical Touch:	12
Words of Affirmation:	7
Quality Time:	6
Acts of Service:	4
Receiving Gifts:	1

To translate this for those who have zero experience with love languages, when Glen and his lady spend time together, snuggling on the couch is appealing to me. If she snuggles and tells me nice things, that would appeal to me as well. Her washing my clothes and giving me a gift would speak to me less. That is not to say it wouldn't speak to me, just not as loudly.

Also, when I walk across the room to hug her, this is me *loudly* "saying" love. When I tell her how much I appreciate her, I am saying love in a "conversational" tone. When I give her flowers, I am "whispering" love.

But the beauty of love languages is to know what her love languages are. With this tool, a spouse, a parent, or a friend will know by your own hand the method you prefer to hear love.

Let's run the gamut of discernment first.

Do we know where this came from?

Yes. It came from Gary Chapman, senior pastor at Calvary Baptist Church in Winston-Salem, North Carolina.

Can we test this spirit?

Kind of. To truly do a thorough test, we would need to be

close to Chapman, but he has media all over the place, which allows us to get a decent feel for him.

YouTube Channel	Gary Chapman
Video Title	"Life Lessons and Love Languages" Gary Chapman
Publication Date	April 21, 2021
Web Link	https://www.youtube.com/ watch?v=8wl_xJbxHpY

So this came from a pastor, right? It has to be the best thing since sliced bread, right? Right?

Well, I have some bad news, folks.

Take it from a man who has been divorced twice and did his best to master speaking his partner's love language. This love languages thing is *not* the trick. This can help couples be more intentional in showing kindness, but it *cannot* by itself help or save a rough marriage (it was another therapist's recommendation).

In fact, I have a few problems with this system.

I took the love languages test several times throughout one year, and each time the numbers were different. It is completely based on my current mood and the amount of love I am feeling—or rather *not* feeling.

Theoretically, if I could have somehow done a mind-wipe every four hours, I would be willing to bet that even over the course of a day, my numbers are constantly moving.

Statistically, the issue with this is that I know men.

If you tell us that our wife is a 10 for receiving gifts and then a week later tell us she is now a 10 for words of affirmation, we will get frustrated because we thought we had the work of loving a woman turned into a mindless equation. All I have to do is buy her flowers every Monday, and she will always be full of love.

I believe every woman reading this can see the problems with it. A woman goes through a *wide* array of emotions throughout a week, and it is all about timing and relationship. One week it is that loving thing you said, and the next it is that thoughtful gift. Another week it was just cuddling and watching *NCIS*. She doesn't want a formula; she wants actual attunement. She wants a personal relationship with the leader of her family, not to be treated like employee #456677 who gets her check every other Friday.

The five love languages are fantastic when it comes to broadening our minds to see the different ways to show love. It can also stimulate some really good conversations that will inspire growth, but as a tool, it should be used sparingly—very sparingly, my brothers and sisters.

Where is your scripture, Glen? You always have some sneaky verse to back it up, some obscure scripture at the bottom of the ninth.

Yes, I do, family.

God said:

Husbands, love your wives, as Christ loved the church and gave himself up for her,

—Eph. 5:25 ESV

Likewise, wives, be subject to your own husbands, so that even if some do not obey the word, they may be won without a word by the conduct of their wives,

—1 Pet. 3:1 ESV

Gary Chapman says there are only five ways to show and receive love, and you must know yours and hers to do it right (obviously this is my interpretation of his view, but it is close).

Here is one shining, bright, glaring difference.

Those whom I love, I reprove and discipline, so be zealous and repent.

—Rev. 3:19 ESV

These are the words of Christ—*talking to the churches.*

Which love language do you think Chapman would assign rebuking and disciplining your wife to?

Would it be acts of kindness?

Chapman's view, in my opinion, is the hippie version of Christ. His love languages only capture the hippie version of love. Remember, God loved and still loves Israel. And what has he allowed them to go through for the past 1,000 years? Love is different from kindness.

We are from God. Whoever knows God listens to us; whoever is not from God does not listen to us. By this we know the Spirit of truth and the spirit of error. Beloved, let us love one another, for love is from God, and whoever loves has been born of God and knows God. Anyone who does not love does not know God, because God is love.

—1 John 4:6–8 ESV

Dr. Chapman, I do not dream that you would ever see these words in this book, but in case you do, I beg of you to do the following. Change the name to *Kindness Languages*. It breaks the borders of "love" and opens up a whole separate realm of the word *kindness*. If this happens, I would retract my "hippie Christ" statement. I would wholeheartedly agree with you, sir, that these are perfect ways to demonstrate *kindness*.

But as it stands, you are misleading the flock into thinking that love is only time, gifts, hugs, favors, and pretty words. It is confusing the congregation about love, God, and how we are to treat our spouses.

Once the name is changed, the next thing I would recommend is to repent of this.

Not many of you should become teachers, my brothers, for you know that we who teach will be judged with greater strictness.

—James 3:1 ESV

Therefore let us not pass judgment on one another any longer, but rather decide never to put a stumbling block or hindrance in the way of a brother.

—Rom. 14:13 ESV

And for those who would say that I am disobeying the first part of Romans 14:13, that would be an error. I am following my God's direction perfectly in this regard.

Do not admit a charge against an elder except on the evidence of two or three witnesses. As for those who persist in sin, rebuke them in the presence of all, so that the rest may stand in fear.

—1 Tim. 5:19–20 ESV

1. He is an elder at a church, and you (if only in this book) have seen the evidence that I am calling forth the entire body of Christ to review.

2. Open your local search engine and type in any of the following:

"Stop using the five love languages"
"Why the five love languages are harmful"
"Everything wrong with the five love languages"
"Five love languages are not biblical"

Dr./pastor/author/Christian/brother Chapman has already been notified and is persisting in sin. He has already been massively and loudly rebuked by both Christians and therapists alike. The information is all over the media in which he is a major player. This is his realm. If he hasn't seen it, it is because he intentionally chooses not to look.

None of us are perfect, Brother Chapman—most of all me. I got something from this ministry, but it either needs to be changed or thrown into the fire. It is misleading Christian couples. Please repent, brother. It can be a great tool *under* the Bible, but as it stands, it's in contrast to the Bible.

Myers-Briggs: Next on the Menu

As most of my friends and family could have predicted, I am ENTP—debater—but I have some bad news, folks.

Second verse, same as the first, a little bit louder, but a whole lot worse.

Here's the same disclaimer. I am only lifting up this single work.

YouTube Channel	Doreen Virtue
Video Title	"Why the Myers-Briggs Is Just as Bad as the Enneagram"
Publication Date	April 27, 2021
Web Link	https://www.youtube.com/watch?v=M2uHO4cHSpE

Again, I strongly recommend you watch her video, and if you like it, hit the thumbs up button, and leave her a comment.

P.S. Below are my personal notes on her video, so please forgive their scatterbrained nature.

Doreen Virtue

Qualifies herself. Enneagram. Myers-Briggs. Rooted in occultism. Origin: woman in Michigan. Fan of Carl Jung; occultist, séances, channeling, answers from within. Completely cooked up by two home-schooled ladies. Trans-channeling. More Enneagram. *Praise Jesus*, I like this lady. She personally recounts her channelings prior to Christ. Good God, thank you. Addresses feelings. Quotes a lot of the Bible. Wow! The clip has Enneagram creator admitting he used auto-writing to conjure the specific types. Personality tests in general. Recommend MMPI test (science-based). Caution with that. Secular. Not to be used in a church setting.

So, there you go, folks. Just for continuity, I will run the gamut again. Sorry for repeating myself, but I want to make sure that *Enough Chaos*'s opinion is crystal clear.

Beware of false prophets, who come to you in sheep's clothing but inwardly are ravenous wolves. You will recognize them by their fruits. Are grapes gathered from thornbushes, or figs from thistles? So, every healthy tree bears good fruit, but the diseased tree bears bad fruit. A healthy tree cannot bear bad fruit, nor can a diseased tree bear good fruit. Every tree that does not bear good fruit is cut down and thrown into the fire. Thus you will recognize them by their fruits.

—Matt. 7:15–20 ESV

God told me in 1 John 4 to test all spirits. My Christian sister has presented evidence that Myers-Briggs came from communicating with spirits. I cannot confirm that the originator did, in fact, test the spirits, nor can I even confirm that the author was a Christian. If it was from God, it would be considered new scripture. That is not the biggest hiccup in the logic of calling this scripture. The biggest hiccup is that it looks *nothing* like anything Christ has ever said to anyone in the Bible.

So it came from an unknown source and looks nothing like Christ's previous words.

Boil it down.

What can you lose if you throw this tool away? You lose nothing except this seemingly harmless tool, right?

What can you lose if you embrace this tool? You have no clue because you cannot see all the spiderwebs of the darkness. Just like we were tricked in the Garden of Eden with Satan's fancy words, this could be a fancy trick too. It tastes good, but it sours the stomach.

You have a sister who has done a lot of research into its origins. You might want to give it a listen before you make the wrong decision.

P.S. Thank you, ma'am, for all the hard work. If you agree, you might want to let her know on her YouTube platform.

If your church is embracing Myers-Briggs, feel free to take a copy of this book to your pastor and ask him to read this section. Then ask him to explain how much research he has conducted into the origins of Myers-Briggs.

When he says it was recommended by a friend or that he saw another church doing it, please re-ask the question because clearly, the pastor didn't understand the question.

Feel free to show him these verses.

Not many of you should become teachers, my brothers, for you know that we who teach will be judged with greater strictness.

—James 3:1 ESV

But whoever causes one of these little ones who believe in me to sin, it would be better for him to have a great millstone fastened around his neck and to be drowned in the depth of the sea.

—Matt. 18:6 ESV

She said, "No one, Lord." And Jesus said, "Neither do I condemn you; go, and from now on sin no more."

—John 8:11 ESV

It is up to you whether to apply this:

Do not admit a charge against an elder except on the evidence of two or three witnesses. As for those who persist in sin, rebuke them in the presence of all, so that the rest may stand in fear.

—1 Tim. 5:19–20 ESV

Flag Page (aka Laugh Your Way to a Better Marriage)

My family, I challenge you to do this one yourself. I have just literally shown you discernment practices and taken on three giants. I challenge you to do this one.

Mark Gungor – Laugh Your Way to a Better Marriage

Part 1: 2 hours and 8 minutes

Part 2: 2 hours and 33 minutes

I put both of these on a YouTube playlist on the *Enough Chaos* channel to make it easy for you.

The 4.5-hour seminar has a segment that goes into a personality test for you and your spouse, but it can also be done solo.

Here is the personality test website:

https://www.flagpage.com/

Mark Gungor is a pastor; he is wild:

https://celebrationchurch.tv/about/mark-gungor

Feel free to review his works in the form of a podcast on YouTube or wherever else.

P.S. I am in no way affiliated with Flag Page or Mark Gungor.

By the way, do you want to know what I am?

125: Control   121: Perfect   112: Fun   76: Peace

Soft: 91   Hard: 101

```
+-------------------------------------------+
|                    |                      |
|   OPTIMISTIC       |     IDEALISTIC       |
|           +--------------------+          |
|           |                    |          |
|-----------|  SINCERE AT HEART  |----------|
|           |                    |          |
|           +--------------------+          |
|                    |                      |
|   CREATIVE         |     UNIQUE           |
|                    |                      |
+-------------------------------------------+
```

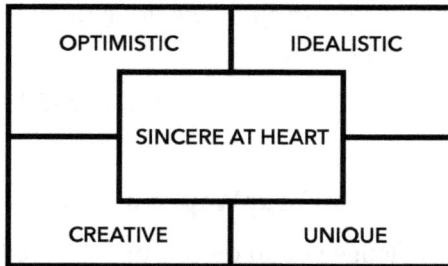

Final Thoughts on Personality Tests:
Here is Opinion 4: *Enough Chaos.*

All or nothing as long as everything stays below the Bible and every tool is in its proper place. Discernment is key.

Don't lean on these personality tests to tell you who you are. They capture a moment in time—a single moment. Tools can help, but they can never do the real work that God, Christ, and the Spirit can do. God tells me who I am, not a program, a website, or a book unless it is the Good Book. Tools should be used, cleaned, and put away lest you grow dependent on them.

ASTROLOGY

This, my family, is one of my favorite chapters I have ever written, but not for the reason most of you are thinking right now.

It is my favorite chapter because I am tired of having the notes all over my phone and hard drive. I took on this subject a little in November 2020, got geared up and hardcore in January 2021, and simmered down in March 2021.

Why is this important to Christians?

It is important because astrology has seeped into our American culture and thus into our Christian culture. I want you to see the truth so you are never pulled by it.

Why is this important for church leadership?

It is important because, for the longest time, church leaders just threw astrology into a trashcan and walked away, abandoning the church members and their feelings and thoughts.

Here is a recounting of an imaginary conversation.

Sally: Hi, Brother Bob (pastor at her church). I have a question for you.

Bob: Sure, Sister Sally. What is it?

Sally: I was reading on the Internet, and it had a silly article that I didn't read, but the headline was "Geminis Will Be Rich This Month."

Bob: You should stay away from mystics, Sister Sally.

Sally: I know, but . . .

Bob: Ms. Sally, you can either choose to believe the Bible or your mystics. That choice is yours.

Bob walks back to his office and shuts the door.

This is exactly how a lot of congregants feel they are treated when they stumble onto astrology and bring it to their church leaders. Was Bob the pastor correct? Yes. Did Bob act shepherd-like? No. He saw a sheep stuck in the fence, said a few words, and abandoned it.

This book will not do that. I have listened and will listen to all your thoughts, theories, and questions and do my best to show you the logic issues as well as the biblical issues.

You are my sister or brother, and I love you, but we need to have a serious talk.

Education: Astrology is different from astronomy.

Astronomy is people looking through a telescope and saying, "Look how pretty that is. I wonder why that star is red versus that other star that is orange. I guess that it has too much radium in its atmosphere." That is astronomy in a very simplified manner—we humans studying the stars.

Astrology is looking into the night sky and believing the heavenly bodies have a direct effect on what happens on earth, including the events that happen in our life.

I am going to present this chapter in four distinct parts.

First, I will discuss the differences in the types of astrology and throw one specific one out on principle alone.

Second, being the debater that I am, I am going to provide all the Bible scripture that astros (my short word for astrologers) use to prop up astrology as being "okay with God." Below each scripture, I will provide the *Enough Chaos* view to counter the astro view.

Third, I will give you my "star-chart" and show you how it could have pulled at me were I not grounded in good scripture and the Holy Spirit. I will openly relay to you how this feels "tasty."

Fourth, I will use the Bible and rightly divide the Word. I will also throw in some dramatic logic points.

Is everybody ready for this? Buckle up, family, because this is going to be a wild ride.

Different Types of Astro

The first and most popular school is solar astrology. When you see your horoscope in the newspaper, online, or on TV, they are referring to solar astrology.

Anything that solely bases things on your birth date is most likely considered solar astrology. This school says that when you were born, there was a dominant sign (constellation) that day and certain energies that coalesced during the forming of you. These energies play a role in your past, current state, and future. This does not imply that it controls you but merely that it influences you.

The second school is the oldest and most seductive. It is what I will call heavenly astrology. This school embraces not only the earth's position to the sun when you were born but also to the moon, Mars, Venus, and everything in the sky.

Just like the belief that the moon affects people on earth, this school believes that everything in the sky affects everything on earth, but the farther away the object is, the less effect it has on the person, especially during birth.

Glen's Dork Session

Science would call this the basic theory of energy, which is that every object is energy. Einstein knew it, and we can prove that everything has energy in it. Take this view, and mix it with a *unique view* of Newton's first law of motion that objects in motion will remain in motion unless acted upon by an equal and opposite force. Squint your eyes just a little and look up into the night sky, and you'll get the modern heavenly astrology theory.

To wrap it all up in a digestible nutshell, Mars has energy and is causing an effect on everything around it. That effect trickles to earth and affects the earth and its inhabitants, especially on the day of your birth. What we have seen and measured is nothing compared to the underlying energy current that exists, and science has only begun to recognize the true energy connecting all things—or dark matter—which is theorized to make up 85 percent of the matter in the universe. That means everything you see right now is only 15 percent of what is there.

Chucking Solar Astrology to the Curb

Everything below came from Google searches and will perfectly demonstrate the insanity of solar astrology. This information continues from this source until I end with another callout.

According to Native American astrology, my spirit animal, my solar astrology animal that best identifies my sign personality is the wolf.

According to Greek solar astrology, I am a Pisces, which means my sign is the fish. Remember, sharks are fish too.

According to one site, my animal is a deer. On another, my animal is a rabbit, and even on another, it is a seahorse.

Note: End Google search.

Who is right?

Better yet, let's look at US presidents.

Oh yeah, boy! Let's pull some actual data into the equation instead of relying on theories to paint our reality. What a novel notion! If anyone has ever wondered what I mean when I say I have a statistical mind, I am going to give you a small demonstration. Grab yourself a Coke, get comfy, and enjoy the show.

According to Greek astrology, Pisces people are pushovers, lucky, pretty, natural empaths, and tend to just go with the flow. Take another sign, one that is more dominating, and shouldn't we be able to see a lot more of these types of people in the corporate world and politics—people who are hungry for power, money, fame, and riches?

Pisces people are, according to a ton of sources, compassionate, intuitive, vague, vulnerable, easily hurt by criticism, withdrawn, self-pitying, too caring, generous, and emotional.

I pulled all this information from a website called *Business Insider*. If you as an old-school Christian think this hocus-pocus nonsense is just weird cat ladies and freaks in the woods, you are literally an ancient human whose brain was frozen 50 years ago. Astrology has seeped into every part of our modern culture, including business practices.

https://www.businessinsider.com/zodiac-signs-us-presi
dents-2018-6#some-of-the-most-controversial-presidents-
have-been-capricorns-13

Here are the Greek solar signs for all the presidents,
organized by sign.

Sign	President	Office Number	Birth Date
Aries	Thomas Jefferson	03	13Apr1943
Aries	John Tyler	10	29Mar1790
Taurus	James Monroe	05	28Apr1758
Taurus	James Buchanan	15	23Apr1791
Taurus	Ulysses S. Grant	18	27Apr1822
Gemini	Harry S. Truman	33	8May1884
Gemini	John F. Kennedy	35	29May1917
Gemini	George H. W. Bush	41	12Jun1924
Gemini	Donald Trump	45	14Jun1946
Cancer	John Quincy Adams	06	11Jul1767
Cancer	Calvin Coolidge	30	04Jul1872
Cancer	Gerald Ford	38	14Jul1913
Cancer	George W. Bush	43	06Jul 1946
Leo	Benjamin Harrison	23	20Aug1833
Leo	Herbert Hoover	31	10Aug1874
Leo	Bill Clinton	42	19Aug1946
Leo	Barack Obama	44	04Aug1961
Virgo	William Howard Taft	27	15Sep1857
Virgo	Lyndon B. Johnson	36	27Aug1908
Libra	Rutherford B. Hayes	19	14Oct1822
Libra	Chester A. Arthur	21	05Oct1829
Libra	Dwight D. Eisenhower	34	14Oct1890
Libra	Jimmy Carter	39	01Oct1924

Sign	President	Office Number	Birth Date
Scorpio	John Adams	02	30Oct1735
Scorpio	James Polk	11	02Nov1795
Scorpio	James A. Garfield	20	19Nov1831
Scorpio	Theodore Roosevelt	26	27Oct1858
Scorpio	Warren G. Harding	29	2Nov1865
Scorpio	Joe Biden	46	20Nov1942
Sagittarius	Martin Van Buren	08	05Dec1782
Sagittarius	Zachary Taylor	12	24Nov1784
Sagittarius	Franklin Pierce	14	23Nov1804
Capricorn	Millard Filmore	13	07Jan1800
Capricorn	Andrew Johnson	17	29Dec1808
Capricorn	Woodrow Wilson	28	28Dec1856
Capricorn	Richard Nixon	37	09Jan1913
Aquarius	William Henry Harrison	09	09Feb1773
Aquarius	Abraham Lincoln	16	12Feb1809
Aquarius	William McKinley	25	29Jan1843
Aquarius	Franklin D. Roosevelt	32	30Jan1882
Aquarius	Ronald Reagan	40	06Feb1911
Pisces	George Washington	01	22Feb1732
Pisces	James Madison	04	16Mar 1751
Pisces	Andrew Jackson	07	15Mar1767
Pisces	Grover Cleveland	22,24	18Mar1837

So achieving the highest, most prestigious office in the United States doesn't seem to have a personal pattern, meaning their personal birth date affects their drive to become the most powerful person in the free world.

What about the universe design? We elect a president every four years, right? If the universe were playing fair, maybe there is a pattern there regarding birthdates. Keep in mind that many presidents served two terms, and that will be included too.

Sign	President	Office Number	Birth Date
Pisces	George Washington	01	22Feb1732
Pisces	George Washington	01	22Feb1732
Scorpio	John Adams	02	30Oct1735
Aries	Thomas Jefferson	03	13Apr1943
Aries	Thomas Jefferson	03	13Apr1943
Pisces	James Madison	04	16Mar 1751
Pisces	James Madison	04	16Mar 1751
Taurus	James Monroe	05	28Apr1758
Taurus	James Monroe	05	28Apr1758
Cancer	John Quincy Adams	06	11Jul1767
Pisces	Andrew Jackson	07	15Mar1767
Pisces	Andrew Jackson	07	15Mar1767
Sagittarius	Martin Van Buren	08	05Dec1782
Aquarius	William Henry Harrison	09	09Feb1773
Aquarius	William Henry Harrison	09	09Feb1773
Aries	John Tyler	10	29Mar1790
Aries	John Tyler	10	29Mar1790
Scorpio	James Polk	11	02Nov1795
Scorpio	James Polk	11	02Nov1795
Sagittarius	Zachary Taylor	12	24Nov1784
Sagittarius	Zachary Taylor	12	24Nov1784
Capricorn	Millard Filmore	13	07Jan1800
Capricorn	Millard Filmore	13	07Jan1800
Sagittarius	Franklin Pierce	14	23Nov1804
Sagittarius	Franklin Pierce	14	23Nov1804

Sign	President	Office Number	Birth Date
Taurus	James Buchanan	15	23Apr1791
Taurus	James Buchanan	15	23Apr1791
Aquarius	Abraham Lincoln	16	12Feb1809
Aquarius	Abraham Lincoln	16	12Feb1809
Capricorn	Andrew Johnson	17	29Dec1808
Capricorn	Andrew Johnson	17	29Dec1808
Taurus	Ulysses S. Grant	18	27Apr1822
Taurus	Ulysses S. Grant	18	27Apr1822
Libra	Rutherford B. Hayes	19	14Oct1822
Libra	Rutherford B. Hayes	19	14Oct1822
Scorpio	James A. Garfield	20	19Nov1831
Scorpio	James A. Garfield	20	19Nov1831
Libra	Chester A. Arthur	21	05Oct1829
Libra	Chester A. Arthur	21	05Oct1829
Pisces	Grover Cleveland	22	18Mar1837
Leo	Benjamin Harrison	23	20Aug1833
Pisces	Grover Cleveland	24	18Mar1837
Aquarius	William McKinley	25	29Jan1843
Aquarius	William McKinley	25	29Jan1843
Scorpio	Theodore Roosevelt	26	27Oct1858
Scorpio	Theodore Roosevelt	26	27Oct1858
Virgo	William Howard Taft	27	15Sep1857
Capricorn	Woodrow Wilson	28	28Dec1856
Capricorn	Woodrow Wilson	28	28Dec1856
Scorpio	Warren G. Harding	29	2Nov1865
Scorpio	Warren G. Harding	29	2Nov1865
Cancer	Calvin Coolidge	30	04Jul1872
Cancer	Calvin Coolidge	30	04Jul1872

Sign	President	Office Number	Birth Date
Leo	Herbert Hoover	31	10Aug1874
Aquarius	Franklin D. Roosevelt	32	30Jan1882
Aquarius	Franklin D. Roosevelt	32	30Jan1882
Gemini	Harry S. Truman	33	8May1884
Gemini	Harry S. Truman	33	8May1884
Libra	Dwight D. Eisenhower	34	14Oct1890
Libra	Dwight D. Eisenhower	34	14Oct1890
Gemini	John F. Kennedy	35	29May1917
Virgo	Lyndon B. Johnson	36	27Aug1908
Virgo	Lyndon B. Johnson	36	27Aug1908
Capricorn	Richard Nixon	37	09Jan1913
Capricorn	Richard Nixon	37	09Jan1913
Cancer	Gerald Ford	38	14Jul1913
Libra	Jimmy Carter	39	01Oct1924
Aquarius	Ronald Reagan	40	06Feb1911
Aquarius	Ronald Reagan	40	06Feb1911
Gemini	George H. W. Bush	41	12Jun1924
Leo	Bill Clinton	42	19Aug1946
Leo	Bill Clinton	42	19Aug1946
Cancer	George W. Bush	43	06Jul 1946
Cancer	George W. Bush	43	06Jul 1946
Leo	Barack Obama	44	04Aug1961
Leo	Barack Obama	44	04Aug1961
Gemini	Donald Trump	45	14Jun1946
Scorpio	Joe Biden	46	20Nov1942

Now, because that was a lot of information on multiple pages, I will chew it up a little for you and put it into a digestible manner.

Here is one way to see the data.

Pisces Pisces Scorpio Aries Aries Pisces Pisces Taurus Taurus Cancer Pisces Pisces Sagittarius Aquarius Aquarius Aries Aries Scorpio Scorpio Sagittarius Sagittarius Capricorn Capricorn Sagittarius Sagittarius Taurus Taurus Aquarius Aquarius Capricorn Capricorn Taurus Taurus Libra Libra Scorpio Scorpio Libra Libra Pisces Leo Pisces Aquarius Aquarius Scorpio Scorpio Virgo Capricorn Capricorn Scorpio Scorpio Cancer Cancer Leo Aquarius Aquarius Gemini Gemini Libra Libra Gemini Virgo Virgo Capricorn Capricorn Cancer Libra Aquarius Aquarius Gemini Leo Leo Cancer Cancer Leo Leo Gemini Scorpio

Here is another way to view the data.

Aries = A	Taurus = T	Gemini = G
Cancer = C	Leo = L	Virgo = V
Libra = B	Scorpio = S	Sagittarius = U
Capricorn = O	Aquarius = Q	Pisces = P

PPSAAPPTTCPPUUQQAASSUUOOUUTTQQOOTTB BSSBBPLPQQSSVOOSSCCLQQGGBBGVVOOCBQQG LLCCLLGS

What makes the most sense to me is this:

Aries 4	Taurus 6	Gemini 5	Cancer 6
Leo 6	Virgo 3	Libra 7	Scorpio 10
Sagittarius 5	Capricorn 8	Aquarius 10	Pisces 8

Taking all manners of organizing the data into account, we can deduce the following:

George W. Bush really was a cancer (just a joke, people).

Eisenhower and Carter should have been similar people with similar effects. Anyone who does even a smidgeon of research into these two men will find that to be a complete farce.

Clinton and Obama were both Leos, so they were the same, right? No. They were from the same party and had some similar views, but do the research yourself. They spoke differently, handled their lives differently, and married dramatically different women.

Being a Gemini president means you will only do a single term.

Kennedy was assassinated in his first term, George H. W. Bush lost his reelection to Clinton, and Trump lost his reelection to Biden.

Gemini means only one term. Truman was a fluke.

Take any top 10 most-liked presidents in history, use whatever source you like, and see what you get.

Here is what I got.

Aquarius Gemini Pisces Scorpio Aries Libra **Aquarius** Leo **Aquarius** Gemini

So Aquarius people tend to leave better tastes in people's mouths long after their office terms are over.

Oops! Wait a minute. Put that statistic next to assassinations.

Aquarius Scorpio **Aquarius** Gemini

Fifty percent of US presidents who were assassinated were Aquarius, for those people not good with math.

Add in failed attempts and shootings.

Pisces **Aquarius** Scorpio **Aquarius** Scorpio **Aquarius** Gemini Gemini Cancer **Aquarius**

So they leave lasting impressions, both good and bad.

That line of reasoning went nowhere. Here are some other lines of reasoning that are all over the place.

Impeached:

Capricorn Leo **Gemini Gemini**

Started Wars:

Pisces Scorpio **Aquarius** Capricorn **Aquarius**

Started Undeclared Wars:

Scorpio Aries Pisces **Taurus Taurus Capricorn Capricorn** Libra Virgo Aquarius Gemini **Cancer Cancer** (three-way tie)

Finished Wars:

Pisces Scorpio **Aquarius** Capricorn **Aquarius**

US Debt to Zero:

Pisces

The fact that the only US president to get the national debt to zero was a Pisces should scream out to everyone who believes in solar astrology that there is a major flaw in your beliefs.

For those who don't understand, Pisces are known for being bad with money—horrible.

Let's just destroy solar astrology once and for all.

Some famous Pisces people are Justin Bieber and Albert Einstein.

Let that sink in, folks. I want you to imagine the conversation between these two men. Justin Bieber and Albert Einstein are both supposed to have the same energy signatures.

How about this: Steve Jobs and John Wayne Gacy (the serial killer).

Actually, how about Justin Bieber, Albert Einstein, Steve Jobs, John Wayne Gacy, Rihanna, Emily Blunt, Floyd Mayweather, Eva Mendes, Rashida Jones, Daniel Craig, George Washington, Sidney Poitier, Jessica Biel, Chelsea Handler, Dr. Seuss, Kristin Davis, Steph Curry, Kurt Cobain, Carrie Underwood, Steve Irwin, Adam Levine, Smokey Robinson, Seal, Drew Barrymore, Dakota Fanning, Jon Bon Jovi, James Van Der Beek, Shaquille O'Neal, Mr. Rogers, Queen Latifa, Oscar Isaac, and Bryan Cranston.

Please tell me that you all see how ludicrous this is.

Keep in mind, family, that I haven't even taken the issue to Daddy yet, and I have shown direct statistics that do not point to a person's solar sign having anything to do with their intelligence, their personality, their future, or what jobs they might be good at.

Want more proof? The funniest video to destroy this view is on YouTube. A self-professed astrologer tries to guess people's solar signs by seeing the person and asking them two or three questions.

YouTube Channel	Cut
Video Title	"An Astrologer Guesses Strangers' Zodiac Sign (Ray)" | Lineup | Cut
Publication Date	February 27, 2018
Web Link	https://www.youtube.com/watch?v=rd-yH8hzTLs

Eight of 12 wrong.
Here is another.

https://www.youtube.com/watch?v=twYPgc92WCI

Four of six wrong.
And another.

https://www.youtube.com/watch?v=56apAKzl0uc

Five of six wrong.

These are supposed to be professional, 100-percent-of-their-job astrologers. There is an additional thing here. I will mention it when we get to the end of the next section. But these astrologers put themselves and their abilities (within their belief structure) to the test and wouldn't have made a passing grade in any school across the land with their results.

How about we go back to me as an example. I am a Pisces, right? We are known for being the least educated and worst in school, right?

Here is me opening my life up to you all so you can see the truth. I am not bragging. I am giving you the truth.

1999 – High School Diploma

2000 – Marine Corps Recruit Depot 3mon

2000 – Marine Combat Training 2wk

2000 – Aviation Machinist's Mate Course A1 C6012013 1mon

2001 – F-402-RR-408A IMA C-601-3893A 6mon (turbojets)

2001 – Naval Aviation Dispersed Technical Publications Librarian 30hr

2001 – MOL Fundamentals of Marine Corps Leadership 26hrs

2001 – MOL Theory & Construction of Turbine Engine 19hrs

2002 – Hazwaste Training 40hr

2002 – Flight line Spill Clean-Up Requirements 30hr

2002 – MOL Personal Finance Management 7hrs

2002 – MOL Basic Nutrition 12hrs

2002 – MOL Spelling 16hrs

2002 – MOL Counseling for Marines 8hrs

2002 – MOL Terrorism Awareness for Marines 8hrs

2002 – MOL Intro to Marine Corps Accounting 12hrs

2002 – MOL Basic Warehousing 14hrs

2002 – MOL Introduction to Test Equipment 3hrs

2002 – MOL Marine Electrician 18hrs

2003 – Hazwaste Refresher 8hr

2003 – MC Corporals Course

2003 – MOL Math for Marines 1334 22hrs

2003 – MOL Legal Admin Clerk 10hrs

2003 – MOL 0119G Punctuation 15hrs

2003 – MOL Warfighting Techniques 7hrs

2003 – MOL Weapons 20hrs

2003 – MOL Aviation Maintenance Workcenter Supervisor 21hrs

2003 – MOL Introduction to Combat Intelligence 18hrs

2003 – MOL Intelligence Brief: Southwest Asia 16hrs

2003 – MOL 1143 Interior Wiring 19hrs

2003 – MOL Solid State Devices 17hrs

2003 – MOL 1332G Metal Working & Welding Operations 21hrs

2004 – 3d MAW Nuclear, Biological Chemical Defense School

2004 – MOL 303H Warehousing Operations 22hrs

2005 – Real Estate Principles 1 30hr

2005 – Laws of Agency 1111 30hr

2005 – Commercial Real Estate 0531 30hr

2005 – Real Estate Principles 2 0112 30hr

2005 – Laws of Contracts 1200 30hr

2005 – TDCJ Correctional Officer 0111 30dy

2006 – US Army Combat Life Saver 40hr

2008 – Escape System Training (Offshore) 4hr

2008 – Basic Offshore Safety Induction Huet&EBS Escape 40hr

2008 – Helicopter Underwater Egress 8hr

2008 – Human Machine Interface AMH Equipment

2009 – SAP Basics 30hr

2010 – Hazardous Waste Accumulation Point Training 40hr

2011 – OSHA30 General Industry

2011 – OSHA30 Construction

2011 – Fall Protection User 4hr

2011 – Confined Space Entry 4hr

2014 – International CPR Institute

2015 – OSHA 0510 Occupational Safety & Health Standards for Construction Industry 31hrs

2015 – OSHA 3115 Fall Protection 23hrs

2016 – Tool Watch Essential Course 8hr

2016 – Tool Watch Enterprise Mobile and Services & Calibration Course 4hr

2017 – Forklift Train-the-Trainer 4hr

2019 – OSHA 0500 Trainer Course in OSHA Standards for Construction 30hrs

2019 – EH1010 English Composition 1 (grade 89)

2019 – SP1010 Speech (grade 98)

2019 – PSY1010 Psychology (grade 88)

2019 – BOS3001 Fundamentals of Occupational Safety & Health (89)

2020 – BOS3525 Legal Aspects of Safety & Health (grade 97)

2020 – FIR3303 Intro to Fire Prevention (grade 94)

2020 – MAT1302 Algebra 1 (grade 92)

2020 – PHL2350 Philosophies of World Religions (grade 100)

2020 – CHM1030 General Chemistry 1 (grade 95)

2020 – BOS1325 Hazardous Materials Management (grade 93)

2020 – OSHA 2015 Hazardous Materials 26hrs

2020 – Authorized First Aid/CPR/AED Instructor

2020 – Authorized OSHA 10 & OSHA 30 Instructor 1926 Construction

2021 – BIO1100 Non-Majors Biology (grade 92)

2021 – OSHA 3095 Electrical Standards 26hrs

2021 – OSHA 0511 Occupational Safety & Health Standards for General Industry 30hrs

2021 – OSHA 0521 OSHA Guide to Industrial Hygiene

2021 – Specialist in Safety & Health (Construction)

2021 – Specialist in Safety & Health (General Industry)

Does that look like someone who is rated "bad" or "worst" in school? Does that look like someone not interested in formal education and learning? No.

I have proven, in my opinion, that classifying someone based on their solar sign is fruitless and errored.

I do think it is interesting how many Pisces are on the serial killer list, though.

Remember, folks, it is all or nothing. It is either good fruit from a good tree or it is not. I believe I have *fully* demonstrated that this solar astrology belief is not only disprovable but the reasoning is from a Pisces person who is supposed to be wishy-washy. And he's writing this book you are reading right now.

Either way, let's move on.

Heavenly Astrology, Come on Down!

When I first was urged to address the topic of astrology, I only knew about solar astrology. So I figured it would be cut and dried, nice and easy, and then I stumbled on heavenly astrology, and holy moly, I realized I was in for a real task. I realized the scope of what I was called to do. I realized why God called me to do this specific task—me specifically.

Below is my entire astrology chart, or natal chart.

Area/Heavenly Body	Sign	Area of Effect
Sun	Pisces	Main concerns, ego
Moon	Capricorn	Emotions
Mercury	Pisces	Intellect, communication
Venus	Taurus	Love
Mars	Leo	Action, primal instincts
Jupiter	Virgo	Freedom, optimism
Saturn	Virgo	Restriction, pessimism
Uranus	Scorpio	Rebellion
Neptune	Sagittarius	Imagination
Pluto	Libra	Obsession, power
Rising Sign	Gemini	Social interaction
North Node	Leo	Karmic path forward
South Node	Aquarius	Previous path, past lives
1st	Gemini	Self-awareness, projection to others
2nd	Cancer	Resourcefulness, values
3rd	Leo	Speaking and writing style
4th	Leo	Home life, foundation

Area/Heavenly Body	Sign	Area of Effect
5th	Libra	Creativity, romance
6th	Scorpio	Self-improvement, health
7th	Sagittarius	Marriage, one-on-one, relationships
8th	Capricorn	Growth, change
9th	Aquarius	Philosophy
10th	Aquarius	Career, achievement
11th	Aries	Clubs, friendships
12th	Taurus	Service, sacrifice

For most Christians, this chart looks like a bunch of random words on a mumbo-jumbo chart similar to the 25-cent fortune-telling game at the arcade when we were kids. But to someone steeped in astrology, this chart speaks to them.

Here are some of the deductions they could pull from looking at the chart.

We have already destroyed Pisces Sun in the previous section. I will not dwell on that further.

I have a Capricorn Moon, which means my heart is mature and austere. My heart is a closed-door, tightly closed, and safe. My emotions are very controlled and methodical. Emotionally, I'm a very serious person and seldom let out my emotions.

Problem 1: Anyone who knows me knows that I am usually, emotionally speaking, in a very happy place. I show it. I walk around singing or humming. I smile and laugh out loud. The big one is that I don't feel embarrassed to show my emotions.

This one is out.

I have a Mercury in Pisces, which is communication. For the untrained person, let me elaborate. I am supposed to be very flighty, spiritual, and deep with my communications, as well as aloof with almost a mystical depth.

Problem 2: I am an ADHD scatterbrain sometimes, but I can and have led safety briefings for 400 construction workers for more than 20 minutes. I know very well how to speak in public. I am articulate and excellent on my feet. I am not prone to jitters unless I don't know the topic. I also excel at tribunal and firing squad types of public interactions with little or no prep. I am very factual and would rather admit I do not know something than quote something wrong or lie.

This Mercury Pisces situation does not match me, not even a little.

I am not going to go through the rest with you, but I do have the results of my findings.

I talked to five of my friends: three Christians and two agnostics. I got their information, filled out their natal chart information, went online and found a less-than-30-minute video on their moon signs, and sent it to each person.

I asked them this simple question: "Would you say the video captured you?"

All five said no. All five also laughed at me for making them do this.

P.S. Thanks again, TS, KC, TC, JL, and TL.

In the interest of honest confession, I did find a video about Leo Mars that spoke a little to me. Its lure was present. It was calling to me, but I did not give in. I am my father's adopted son, and I will never kneel to a statue.

The Bible's calling through the Holy Spirit inside of me speaks loudly and honestly. The calling to this was seductive and quiet. When you have seen the need for light, the darkness cannot find a place.

Again, family, after destroying solar astrology, mixed with my own research and my five guinea pig experiments, and without even using my Father's Word, I have dispelled this entire myth and practice.

It is either all in or all out. It is either good or bad. We cannot as Christians afford to be wrong here.

So now that I have done my cute little song and dance, let's bring in the only opinion that really matters—God's opinion from the Good Book.

Astrologers' Thoughts

Claim 1: God made the stars for us to see and know what to do and what was coming. It's just like the wise men who followed the Star of Bethlehem to Jesus.

> *And God said, "Let there be lights in the expanse of the heavens to separate the day from the night. And let them be for signs and for seasons, and for days and years.*
>
> —Gen. 1:14 ESV

> *After listening to the king, they went on their way. And behold, the star that they had seen when it rose went before them until it came to rest over the place where the child was.*
>
> —Matt. 2:9 ESV

Claim 2: Astrology is in the Bible. Didn't the book of Job refer to the constellations?

Enough Chaos response: yes, but not just in Job.
Who made the Bear and Orion,
the Pleiades and the chambers of the south.

—Job 9:9 ESV

Can you bind the chains of the Pleiades
or loose the cords of Orion?
Can you lead forth the Mazzaroth in their season,
or can you guide the Bear with its children?

—Job 38:31–32 ESV

He who made the Pleiades and Orion,
and turns deep darkness into the morning
and darkens the day into night,
who calls for the waters of the sea
and pours them out on the surface of the earth,
the Lord is his name;

—Amos 5:8 ESV

And a great sign appeared in heaven: a woman clothed
with the sun, with the moon under her feet, and on her
head a crown of twelve stars.

—Rev. 12:1 ESV

Constellations are all throughout the Bible. John didn't know the term Virgo, so he didn't use the words that would have made it clear to us. He described what he saw. He saw planets moving in the constellation Virgo. John says a sign "appeared in heaven." He looked up and saw a sign.

Rick Larson does a phenomenal presentation called "Star of Bethlehem," posted on YouTube on November 27,

2015, by Revived Life. https://www.youtube.com/watch?v=exmbuX1NffU

Only God is the master of the stars, but Rick Larson, a regular Joe kind of lawyer from somewhere in America, stumbles upon an idea and gives us all a feast from above just by showing people the stars. Knowledge is greatly multiplied. https://bethlehemstar.com/

Claim 3: Astrology doesn't replace the Bible; it works alongside the Bible. Astrology is just one of the tools God uses to show his love to us.

No, astrology says the stars are in control of events, including our personality types.

I am the Lord, and there is no other,
besides me there is no God;
I equip you, though you do not know me,
that people may know, from the rising of the sun
and from the west, that there is none besides me;
I am the Lord, and there is no other.
I form light and create darkness;
I make well-being and create calamity;
I am the Lord, who does all these things.

—Isa. 45:5–7 ESV

Not planets. Not stars. Not other solar systems. God is in control—God and nothing else.

In Jude, they called the planets "wandering stars."

Wild waves of the sea, casting up the foam of their own
shame; wandering stars, for whom the gloom of utter
darkness has been reserved forever.

—Jude 1:13 ESV

Modern man has given stars a new name: planets. But the Bible clearly calls them stars. When you claim that my actions in any way are dictated by stars, I see that as a form of giving power to the stars. When you say my entire personality, past, and present are dictated by the stars, you are saying the stars are God. You are claiming with your mouth the God that you serve.

My God has given you very direct and specific warnings about worshiping stars. I am not quoting Leviticus, which were rules for the 12 tribes to follow. I am quoting the stories of what God does when he sees his people specifically worship stars.

And beware lest you raise your eyes to heaven, and when you see the sun and the moon and the stars, all the host of heaven, you be drawn away and bow down to them and serve them, things that the Lord your God has allotted to all the peoples under the whole heaven.

—Deut. 4:19 ESV

And he deposed the priests whom the kings of Judah had ordained to make offerings in the high places at the cities of Judah and around Jerusalem; those also who burned incense to Baal, to the sun and the moon and the constellations and all the host of the heavens.

—2 Kings 23:5 ESV

*Now therefore hear this, you lover of pleasures,
who sit securely,
who say in your heart,
"I am, and there is no one besides me;
I shall not sit as a widow*

or know the loss of children":
These two things shall come to you
in a moment, in one day;
the loss of children and widowhood
shall come upon you in full measure,
in spite of your many sorceries
and the great power of your enchantments.
You felt secure in your wickedness;
you said, "No one sees me";
your wisdom and your knowledge led you astray,
and you said in your heart,
"I am, and there is no one besides me."
But evil shall come upon you,
which you will not know how to charm away;
disaster shall fall upon you,
for which you will not be able to atone;
and ruin shall come upon you suddenly,
of which you know nothing.
Stand fast in your enchantments
and your many sorceries,
with which you have labored from your youth;
perhaps you may be able to succeed;
perhaps you may inspire terror.
You are wearied with your many counsels;
let them stand forth and save you,
those who divide the heavens,
who gaze at the stars,
who at the new moons make known
what shall come upon you.
Behold, they are like stubble;
the fire consumes them;
they cannot deliver themselves

from the power of the flame.
No coal for warming oneself is this,
no fire to sit before!
Such to you are those with whom you have labored,
who have done business with you from your youth;
they wander about, each in his own direction;
there is no one to save you.

—Isa. 47:8–15 ESV

Did you bring to me sacrifices and offerings during the forty years in the wilderness, O house of Israel? You shall take up Sikkuth your king, and Kiyyun your star-god—your images that you made for yourselves, and I will send you into exile beyond Damascus, says the Lord, whose name is the God of hosts.

—Amos 5:25–27 ESV

Therefore God gave them up in the lusts of their hearts to impurity, to the dishonoring of their bodies among themselves, because they exchanged the truth about God for a lie and worshiped and served the creature rather than the Creator, who is blessed forever! Amen.

For this reason, God gave them up to dishonorable passions. For their women exchanged natural relations for those that are contrary to nature; and the men likewise gave up natural relations with women and were consumed with passion for one another, men committing shameless acts with men and receiving in themselves the due penalty for their error.

And since they did not see fit to acknowledge God, God gave them up to a debased mind to do what ought not to be done. They were filled with all manner of unrighteousness, evil, covetousness, malice. They are full of envy, murder, strife, deceit, maliciousness. They are gossips, slanderers, haters of God, insolent, haughty, boastful, inventors of evil, disobedient to parents, foolish, faithless, heartless, ruthless. Though they know God's righteous decree that those who practice such things deserve to die, they not only do them but give approval to those who practice them.

—Rom. 1:24–32 ESV

When you take something that God made and give power to it, you are worshiping it and not the Creator. This is how God will see it.

Ignore the truth, and he will give you over to your sins. Your sins will get worse year by year and generation by generation.

Claim 4: The moon affects humans. Emergency rooms, police services, and fire departments across the country see an increase in activity on full moon nights.

There have been many real studies on this, and the answer is no. The main objection here is what about all the nights we see these increases when there aren't full moons? People are people, and coincidences happen. Also, don't forget that God put the moon up there to be a source of light for us. When people have light, they tend to be more active.

Think of it like this. Go outside at 3:00 p.m., and then go outside at 3:00 a.m. Which time is more likely to have more people running around? The time with the light or the time with less light? Now put a full moon in the sky that lights up the night. I'm not saying that is the fact that breaks the case; I am just throwing out another reason some services might see increased frequencies on bright nights other than we are all werewolves being drawn by the goddess Luna.

Here is another scripture that people use to prop up astrology.

> *There is one glory of the sun, and another glory of the moon, and another glory of the stars; for star differs from star in glory.*

—1 Cor. 15:41 ESV

This is *utterly* destroyed when you look at the verse before that and a few below.

> *There are heavenly bodies and earthly bodies, but the glory of the heavenly is of one kind, and the glory of the earthly is of another. There is one glory of the sun, and another glory of the moon, and another glory of the stars; for star differs from star in glory. So is it with the resurrection of the dead. What is sown is perishable; what is raised is imperishable. It is sown in dishonor; it is raised in glory. It is sown in weakness; it is raised in power. It is sown a natural body; it is raised a spiritual body. If there is a natural body, there is also a spiritual body.*

—1 Cor. 15:40–44 ESV

Oh! So it is just saying some stars are brighter than others? No.

It is saying there is a difference between a man's body and his soul. The differences are as different as the ground is to the air, as the moon is from the sun, as the sun is from other suns, as dishonor is from honor, as weakness is from power.

Enough Chaos: Final Thoughts

Do you know the ordinances of the heavens?
Can you establish their rule on the earth?

—Job 38:33 ESV

You need to leave any form of astrology alone.

In my estimation, there's probably a less than 1 percent chance that God has used the planets to do anything. I have no thought that they dictate anything, but could God have some other use for his creations—maybe?

I cannot 100 percent rule it out because I do not know how God designed everything, but I can tell you that based on solar astrology, that is completely not true. Based on our understanding of heavenly astrology, that is completely not true.

I can see a statistic in our personalities and our reactions, but I cannot see its relations to the planets. I can't even really see the statistic itself; it is more of a smell. I see the same person sometimes. There is a different face, a different voice, but the same tendencies. I imagine it is like seeing the smudges on the side of God's glass of creation. I can sense it, but it is completely intangible, and I love him for it.

None of this points me to "everyone with the same moon sign acts the same way" in any way. Again, it is either all or it is nothing because there are so many flaws in our understanding of personalities and space that we cannot embrace this.

It is not based on God's calendar. Maybe someone could sit down with an astronomer (not astrologer) and layout something based on God's calendar, including Adar 2 (yes there is a 13th month that only happens occasionally). Think of it like the Greek calendar's leap year. We use the Greek calendar in America.

And yes, there is a 13th zodiac sign that most people don't know about. It is a giant snake in the sky. Take that information, and lay all of it out. Perform millions of surveys, have actual trustworthy science people, and maybe, just maybe, that might yield a piece of data. But we need to look at cost versus reward. The cost for doing that would be astronomical, and the reward for doing that would be what?

You feeling like you belong somewhere?

You feeling like your emotions and thoughts are not crazy?

You being told that someone born three months from your birthdate could be perfect for you?

You being assigned a job, a house, and a car based on your birth date?

We should be getting all this comfort we search for in personality tests and astrology from God, Jesus, the Holy Spirit, the Bible, and the church body, not from statistical data of things floating in space and not from science. Both of those roads will lead us nowhere.

I am not throwing down science. I love science, but it should never be used to tell us who we are, what our worth is, or what our future holds. All of that is up to God—only *God*.

Don't get me wrong. Some cool facts can pop up like Pisces people are more likely to be serial killers. Maybe there are even some unique trends that could show themselves such as

Aquarius presidents getting shot more than others. But in the end, it is foolish coincidences.

Think of it like this. If I took two people who statistically were supposed to fit together and tried to make them get married, do you really think it would work? Is there any part of you that believes any human on earth can do that?

How about every single human on earth pooling their mental prowess together? Could they get a 100 percent guaranteed match?

No, I don't think that either. But you're going to say that a mindless planet's energy tendrils can create two people who are perfect for each other—like Pisces and Cancer.

This isn't *Moneyball*, the 2011 film with Brad Pitt, where we are predicting the best players for a team based on their performance records, home runs, hits, catches, and so on. This is people's lives, and our lives are messy and sometimes both tragic and glorious. Sometimes we cry, sometimes we laugh, sometimes we do both in the same breath, and you want to reduce that to a calculation based on something that is a bazillion miles away.

The real kicker is where did all these people get their explanations of what star or planet did what? Who told them that the planet Mars influences my tendency to get mad or that my Leo Mars explains my readiness to go to war at a moment's notice.

Again, just like with personality tests, where did this knowledge come from?

Beware of false prophets, who come to you in sheep's clothing but inwardly are ravenous wolves. You will recognize them by their fruits. Are grapes gathered from thornbushes, or figs from thistles? So, every healthy tree bears good fruit, but the diseased tree bears bad fruit. A healthy tree cannot bear bad fruit, nor can a diseased tree bear good fruit. Every tree that does not bear good fruit is cut down and thrown into the fire. Thus you will recognize them by their fruits.

—Matt. 7:15–20 ESV

I have shown you flaws all over astrology. Every single form of astrology is flawed because it comes from a flawed source.

Think of what Satan did in the Garden of Eden.

Now the serpent was more crafty than any other beast of the field that the Lord God had made.

He said to the woman, "Did God actually say, 'You shall not eat of any tree in the garden'?" And the woman said to the serpent, "We may eat of the fruit of the trees in the garden, but God said, 'You shall not eat of the fruit of the tree that is in the midst of the garden, neither shall you touch it, lest you die.'" But the serpent said to the woman, "You will not surely die. For God knows that when you eat of it your eyes will be opened, and you will be like God, knowing good and evil."

—Gen. 3:1–5 ESV

All Satan did was ask questions. He used his fancy tongue and asked a long question that caught Eve in that slow, quiet, seductive whisper. It pulled on her heart, and she fell. Then Adam fell.

But, my family, you do not have to continue living this way.

For if, because of one man's trespass, death reigned through that one man, much more will those who receive the abundance of grace and the free gift of righteousness reign in life through the one man Jesus Christ.

Therefore, as one trespass led to condemnation for all men, so one act of righteousness leads to justification and life for all men. For as by the one man's disobedience the many were made sinners, so by the one man's obedience the many will be made righteous.

—Rom. 5:17–19 ESV

If you are clinging in any way to astrology, please come out of the darkness.

After-Thought

There is only one road I did not get to entertain, and that is where I found a person trying to draw a link between the 12 apostles, the 12 zodiac signs, and the 12 Hebrew months. Paul, the 13th apostle, would be the 13th zodiac Snake and Adar 2.

I cannot find the apostles' birth dates, but I can find plenty of sites that "magically" connect the apostles to a zodiac sign.

Please do not fall into this one either. There is *zero* biblical backing for this.

Think of it this way: which month of the year was Judas the traitor born in?

While he was still speaking, there came a crowd, and the man called Judas, one of the twelve, was leading them. He drew near to Jesus to kiss him, but Jesus said to him, "Judas, would you betray the Son of Man with a kiss?"

—Luke 22:47–48 ESV

Should we treat everyone born in this month like a traitor?
Should we outlaw these people from giving anyone kisses?
How about we permanently attach iron masks to their faces the day they are born?
Exactly.

TAROT AND PSYCHICS

Finally, I get to release this. There is not a single chapter in all my works for the Lord that I have chomped on the bit more to get to write. This is it.

First, why is this so important to me?

Solar astrology was always in my culture, but every time it caught my attention, there were enough errors that I could see through the fog right away, even before I was saved. When God had me start doing this prep, I was kind of confused because I didn't think many Christians fell into the horoscope world, but I trusted God, so okay. I did the research for about a week, and then I stumbled onto heavenly astrology.

I felt the sweet pull of the darkness calling, and I saw it for what it was. Throughout the course of a month, I had that one in the bag, too, but the weight of the mission hadn't lessened. I still had more to go. I looked at Chinese astrology, but that was equally comparable to heavenly astrology. It was certainly more complicated, but it was the same basic idea, from the same unknown source, with the same scripture warning against it.

Then I found tarot.

I felt pulled to it but not that sweet voice drawing me in. This was the butt-kicking force of God pointing me in a direction.

I can almost hear Justin Peters' redneck scholarly voice in my head. I can imagine him looking into the camera at his church and saying, "This man claims that God told him to do tarot. I don't think so. Friends (as he looks to the crowd), this is shocking" (pronounced shawking in his accent).

I love you, Brother Peters, and all the work you do.

So yes, I felt the nudge of God to look here.

The idea of using cards to tell me things just felt silly. It has always felt silly, but I will obey.

I listened to one video and felt nothing.

Then I listened to another . . . and nothing.

Then another and another and another, and to be honest, I was getting a little frustrated. And then I heard it. When I heard it the first time, I was floored. I was dazed. I understood my mission, but I had no clue how far and long it would reach. I had no clue how truly underground this tarot thing was.

For the next three months, I consumed video after video, listening for the specific words they were using, identifying the entities they called upon to guide them, listening to the readers' hearts. I even read a few comments on the pages, and what I saw was deeply, deeply saddening.

So enough about my journey.

I will tell you that if you are a man who has a wife, *please* make, ask, beg her to read this chapter. If you know a Christian female, again, please have this conversation with her. *Please* do not assume she just knows. Please!

There is not a doubt in my mind that there is a very specific darkness out there preying on women, seducing them to this tarot practice. I am not just talking about the Jamaican lady with dreads who lives down in New Orleans and sells occult merchandise. I am talking about housewives. I am talking about soccer moms and businesswomen. The sheer range of women I saw both performing tarot and commenting on the videos spanned the entire spectrum of our American females.

Males, please make sure you have this conversation with your females. There is a spirit of darkness that is hunting them. Female gatherings in the church, please make sure you are addressing this issue with the ladies of your church body. Please do not just old-man-view it. Please unpack *why* it is so dangerous. What is dangerous about it?

At first, I thought this was going to be easy, that I would just throw the no-other-spirits-no-mystics Bible verses up here, just one single page in the book, and move on. But oh, was I a fool! The spirit of darkness in charge of this tarot thing has a slippery tongue. It uses words such as *higher power*, *spirits*, and *divine beings* so they only softly whisper to the user. To most men I know, this wouldn't work because we would rather challenge each other with the cards and play poker.

Without a doubt, this "ability" to get clear guidance from my higher power, this thought, is a seductive one to our relationship-based ladies. It calls to them like a siren on the shores called to Odysseus.

At this point in the chapter, I will switch to talking directly to the tarot person.

First and foremost, every tarot reading I saw called upon a different power to guide the cards. I'm going to break down these and their three main groups.

Group one is ancestors/dead people.

Group two is angelic hosts and archangels.

Group three is God/universe/higher power.

I heard several women accidentally make a mistake and use the word *God* throughout the reading, but every time the word *universe* was used and the way it was used made it clear that they were referring to God.

With this out of the way, let's get to work.

The first one we're going to take on is talking to ancestors/ dead people. The Bible is very clear that the dead are asleep.

> *But we do not want you to be uninformed, brothers, about those who are asleep, that you may not grieve as others do who have no hope. For since we believe that Jesus died and rose again, even so, through Jesus, God will bring with him those who have fallen asleep. For this we declare to you by a word from the Lord, that we who are alive, who are left until the coming of the Lord, will not precede those who have fallen asleep. For the Lord himself will descend from heaven with a cry of command, with the voice of an archangel, and with the sound of the trumpet of God. And the dead in Christ will rise first.*
>
> —1 Thess. 4:13–16 ESV

> *Then he appeared to more than five hundred brothers at one time, most of whom are still alive, though some have fallen asleep.*
>
> —1 Cor. 15:6 ESV

> *But in fact Christ has been raised from the dead, the firstfruits of those who have fallen asleep.*
>
> —1 Cor. 15:20 ESV

> *Behold! I tell you a mystery. We shall not all sleep, but we shall all be changed,*
>
> —1 Cor. 15:51 ESV

This is referring to the ones who will be on earth when Christ returns.

Consider and answer me, O Lord my God;
light up my eyes, lest I sleep the sleep of death.

—Ps. 13:3 ESV

And just as it is appointed for man to die once, and after
that comes judgment.

—Heb. 9:27 ESV

A man dies and falls asleep, and the next thing he knows, he is in judgment.

After saying these things, he said to them, "Our friend
Lazarus has fallen asleep, but I go to awaken him." The
disciples said to him, "Lord, if he has fallen asleep, he
will recover." Now Jesus had spoken of his death, but they
thought that he meant taking rest in sleep. Then Jesus
told them plainly, "Lazarus has died."

—John 11:11–14 ESV

And I heard a voice from heaven saying, "Write this:
Blessed are the dead who die in the Lord from now on."
"Blessed indeed," says the Spirit, "that they may rest from
their labors, for their deeds follow them!"

—Rev. 14:13 ESV

For the living know that they will die, but the dead know
nothing, and they have no more reward, for the memory
of them is forgotten.

—Eccles. 9:5 ESV

Do not marvel at this, for an hour is coming when all who are in the tombs will hear his voice and come out, those who have done good to the resurrection of life, and those who have done evil to the resurrection of judgment.

—John 5:28–29 ESV

And many of those who sleep in the dust of the earth shall awake, some to everlasting life, and some to shame and everlasting contempt.

—Dan. 12:2 ESV

Nowhere in the Bible does it suggest that when you die you get to float around and talk to people and influence things. If any human ancestor spirits are guiding that tarot session, they are in complete defiance of God. You have a defiant spirit guiding the cards. Are you sure you want to trust the advice from this entity?

Do not turn to mediums or necromancers; do not seek them out, and so make yourselves unclean by them: I am the Lord your God.

—Lev. 19:31 ESV

There shall not be found among you anyone who burns his son or his daughter as an offering, anyone who practices divination or tells fortunes or interprets omens, or a sorcerer or a charmer or a medium or a necromancer or one who inquires of the dead, for whoever does these things is an abomination to the Lord. And because of these abominations the Lord your God is driving them out before you.

—Deut. 18:10–12 ESV

And I will cut off sorceries from your hand, and you shall have no more tellers of fortunes;

—Mic. 5:12 ESV

Beloved, do not believe every spirit, but test the spirits to see whether they are from God, for many false prophets have gone out into the world.

—1 John 4:1 ESV

And when they say to you, "Inquire of the mediums and the necromancers who chirp and mutter," should not a people inquire of their God? Should they inquire of the dead on behalf of the living? To the teaching and to the testimony! If they will not speak according to this word, it is because they have no dawn.

—Isa. 8:19–20 ESV

Isaiah is point-blank asking them why they are talking to the dead and spirits. Shouldn't they be talking to God?

And he burned his son as an offering and used fortune-telling and omens and dealt with mediums and with necromancers. He did much evil in the sight of the Lord, provoking him to anger.

—2 Kings 21:6 ESV

The tragic truth is that if the Bible is true and the dead are asleep, then who are these people talking to? Let's review where everyone is who has ever existed.

God = Everywhere

Angels = 1/3 rebelled = thrown to earth

Angels = 2/3 loyal doing God's business in heaven and on earth

Humans, flood and before = bad = hell

Humans, post-flood = dead = asleep waiting judgment

Humans, post-flood = alive = we're still here, homie

So, the terrifying thing is *who* are these people talking to? I have no doubt somebody is giving them advice. Somebody is talking. There are far too many accounts of the spirits providing information about a dead relative or even a past life that checked out.

I touched on this briefly in a previous chapter and said you weren't ready to have the curtain pulled back yet. But now you are. The truth is terrifying. The spirit knows Aunt Sally's favorite color because the spirit was living inside Aunt Sally. The spirit called you Pumpkin, which was your grandpa's nickname for you because the spirit was living inside your grandpa. Which spirits am I referring to? The ones Christ casts out all the time. I am referring to the third of the angels who fell, the angels who can't die, the ones cursed to never be able to ascend to heaven again, the war of the unseen. I beg you, *do not listen to these spirits*. The dead are asleep.

The next group of people are the ones praying to the angelic hosts. The most common prayed to are Archangel Michael, Gabriel, and Metatron. Let me ask you this. Who told you that you had the power to summon angels? Where in the Bible did you get that from? Where in the Bible do we see any examples of a human summoning an angel trick?

We see only one situation where an angel is held, and immediately the next action is Michael the Archangel coming to do battle. That entity who did the holding was Satan. So if you're summoning and holding an angel against its will, the next step is going to be the Archangel Michael coming to do battle against you. Are you sure you want to be summoning angels?

The next thing to think about is just sheer logic. Imagine if you did have the power to summon the Archangel Michael. Just imagine the sheer volume of people who would try to summon Michael in a week. How about a day? How about an hour? He would only be able to be there for about a second, and then he would be summoned to a different person's tarot card reading. You women are summoning that poor dude 700,000 times a day. Wait! Did I say day? I meant literally day and night, day and night.

Do you think maybe the world is going to hell in a handbasket because the only entity assigned to Satan's duty is being summoned so many times a day that he literally can't do his job?

You are making this world bleed so you can find out if your boyfriend is cheating on you or if your boss is conspiring against you.

The primary job of Michael in the Bible is doing battle with Satan.

But when the archangel Michael, contending with the devil, was disputing about the body of Moses, he did not presume to pronounce a blasphemous judgment, but said, "The Lord rebuke you."

—Jude 1:9 ESV

At that time shall arise Michael, the great prince who has charge of your people. And there shall be a time of trouble, such as never has been since there was a nation till that time. But at that time your people shall be delivered, everyone whose name shall be found written in the book.

—Dan. 12:1 ESV

Now war arose in heaven, Michael and his angels fighting against the dragon. And the dragon and his angels fought back, but he was defeated, and there was no longer any place for them in heaven. And the great dragon was thrown down, that ancient serpent, who is called the devil and Satan, the deceiver of the whole world—he was thrown down to the earth, and his angels were thrown down with him.

—Rev. 12:7–9 ESV

Are you sure you want to summon the angel whose job it is to battle Satan? Are you sure that's what you want to release upon the earth? How about we let God be in charge of the Archangel Michael?

So, if you are not summoning an actual angel or an archangel, then who keeps showing up to your tarot readings?

And no wonder, for even Satan disguises himself as an angel of light.

—2 Cor. 11:14 ESV

The coming of the lawless one is by the activity of Satan with all power and false signs and wonders.

—2 Thess. 2:9 ESV

Be sober-minded; be watchful. Your adversary the devil prowls around like a roaring lion, seeking someone to devour.

—1 Pet. 5:8 ESV

But is the devil really that powerful?

And he said to him, "All these I will give you, if you will fall down and worship me."

—Matt. 4:9 ESV

Satan is strong enough to try to tempt Jesus. Also notice that he tempts Christ with everything in sight. That means theoretically he had control of everything in sight from a certain point of view.

Again, I am not saying there is not a spirit at that tarot card reading. I wholeheartedly believe there is an actual spirit descending upon that reading. I have zero doubt. The question is this: who is it?

For we do not wrestle against flesh and blood, but against the rulers, against the authorities, against the cosmic powers over this present darkness, against the spiritual forces of evil in the heavenly places.

—Eph. 6:12 ESV

And another sign appeared in heaven: behold, a great red dragon, with seven heads and ten horns, and on his heads seven diadems. His tail swept down a third of the stars of heaven and cast them to the earth. And the dragon stood before the woman who was about to give birth, so that when she bore her child he might devour it. And the great dragon was thrown down, that ancient serpent, who is called the devil and Satan, the deceiver of the whole world—he was thrown down to the earth, and his angels were thrown down with him.

—Rev. 12:3–4, 9 ESV

Oh, but how many angels were thrown down?

Then I looked, and I heard around the throne and the living creatures and the elders the voice of many angels, numbering myriads of myriads and thousands of thousands,

—Rev. 5:11 ESV

Okay, so this is "around the throne." It is a start, I suppose, but how much is a myriad?

According to Blueletterbible.org, referencing *Strong's Concordance*;

Myriad is;

a. Ten thousand
b. An innumerable multitude, an unlimited number
c. Innumerable hosts

Well, I can't do math up to infinite, so let's take definition 1.

10,000	X	10,000	x	1,000	x	1,000
Myriad		Myriad		Thousands		Thousands

Just doing my garbage math . . .

100,000,000,000,000

If this is the two-thirds who are still left in heaven . . .

$$100,000,000,000,000 / 2 = 50,000,000,000,000$$

So it looks like, *at a minimum*, Satan took 50,000,000,000,000 angels with him down here to earth.

We now call them demons or unclean spirits. Christ dealt with them a lot and put the record of that in the Bible.

The last group is the ones who pray to God, the higher powers, the universe. These are all just fancy ways of saying God, only more disrespectful.

As a Christian, you know you have the power to let the Holy Spirit into you, right? It's through fire baptism, sermon, and opening the door.

Why would you cast out the Holy Spirit (God) from you and then turn around and try to communicate with it (God) through cards? You are literally trying to turn an open conversation with God that you already have into a text conversation using only emojis. And then you're translating that through a tarot card reader. Does that make any sense to you? I even heard one lady call upon Jesus Christ himself to guide the reading.

Jesus Christ is done talking. He spoke to the apostles. They have carried his word throughout the whole world. If you want to get Jesus Christ's words or advice, you will not find them in the cards; you will find them solely in the Bible.

The Bible also contains God's words. Again, you will not find them in the cards; you will find them solely in the Bible.

And you will not find the Holy Spirit's words in the cards; you will find them solely inside of you once you are tuned in, using the Bible.

But the Helper, the Holy Spirit, whom the Father will send in my name, he will teach you all things and bring to your remembrance all that I have said to you.

—John 14:26 ESV

All Scripture is breathed out by God and profitable for teaching, for reproof, for correction, and for training in righteousness, that the man of God may be competent, equipped for every good work.

—2 Tim. 3:16–17 ESV

I am not trying to say that there are not spirits who were controlling those tarot cards. I am 100 percent telling you that it is not the spirit you want to be communicating with. Satan was the most beautiful angel. His voice sounded sweet, but just like a belly full of candy, it will never nourish you. It will suck you dry one way or another. It will string you out just like cocaine.

You have to stop with the mystics.

You have to stop with the throwing of bones.

You have to stop with the rolling of dice.

You have to stop with the tarot cards.

Anything that draws information from an unknown source is not only dangerous, but it directly throws your dependence off of God and onto whatever dark spirit or entity is there ready to pick up the phone. This is not about whether that entity is going to give you good information or bad. This is all about whether that entity is doing what it is supposed to do. Is that entity in line with God, the God of the Bible, the God of salvation, the God of redemption, the God of mercy?

And the answer to that is no because if they are giving you directions through the cards, they are not a good entity to have in your life.

I know you feel alone. I know you feel misunderstood. I know you're worried about the job for the future or your spouse or your boyfriend or your girlfriend or your kids. I know you're worried about these things, but drawing information from evil spirits is not going to help you. It is literally Pandora's box, and the repercussions could be vast and endless. You need to come out of this darkness. Come out right now, please.

You must come out of this darkness cold turkey. Don't wean off of it. You need to separate this connection immediately; it will lead to nothing but ruin.

Unlike personality tests and astrology, this tarot card and psychics thing is directly calling upon spirits. It is very close to the source of darkness. Its voice is so sweet, and its tendrils will wrap around your soul and drag you away from the glory of God. You must come out of this darkness. There are no answers for you on this path that will give you true nourishment.

Your crops will grow, but they will not be fertile. They will be filled with chemicals like a pesticide that has been sprayed on by the darkness, and it will poison all who consume it, change their DNA, and poison their children. This is not a situation where you can take the darkness and use it to your will.

J. R. R. Tolkien wrote a series of books called *The Lord of the Rings*. In this tale, a powerful wizard, Gandalf, refuses to touch the ring of darkness because he knows he cannot take a dark power and bend it to his will.

That is exactly what this is. You do not have that power either. You cannot take a dark power and bend it to your will.

Tarot is communicating with dark powers, and that is just as bad as trying to perform a séance. It's the exact same thing, just with cards.

Submit yourselves therefore to God. Resist the devil, and he will flee from you.

—James 4:7 ESV

Now the Spirit expressly says that in later times some will depart from the faith by devoting themselves to deceitful spirits and teachings of demons, through the insincerity of liars whose consciences are seared, who forbid marriage and require abstinence from foods that God created to be received with thanksgiving by those who believe and know the truth.

—1 Tim. 4:1–3 ESV

Jesus said to him, "I am the way, and the truth, and the life. No one comes to the Father except through me.

—John 14:6 ESV

For there is one God, and there is one mediator between God and men, the man Christ Jesus,

—1 Tim. 2:5 ESV

For the Christian coming out of tarot, if you have been involved in it for any length of time, I can easily predict that you will feel exactly like an addict coming off a drug.

Modern playing cards are 100 percent remnants of previous tarot cards; that might be a trigger. Keep an eye out.

Absolutely, definitely, 100 percent get pastoral care. If you need a support group, find one. I know a lot of pastors' wives who have often led small versions of care groups.

One way or another, you are not alone. You can do this by leaning on God. I believe in you.

MAKING A MARRIAGE WORK

I have prayed and fought with God on whether I should even do this chapter. I feel like a man with *zero* successful marriages should *not* be delivering this topic.

What do you tell a man with two black eyes? *Nothing.* He has already been told twice.

What do you tell a man with two ex-wives? *Nothing.* He ain't listening.

This was my mindset, and then God hit me with a ton of bricks like he always does.

How many wives did Paul have?

Boom! I still don't feel qualified to do this, so I will keep my commentary to a bare minimum. At the very least, I will grab all the verses about marriage and bring them into one chapter.

Therefore a man shall leave his father and his mother and hold fast to his wife, and they shall become one flesh.

—Gen. 2:24 ESV

Put on then, as God's chosen ones, holy and beloved, compassionate hearts, kindness, humility, meekness, and patience, bearing with one another and, if one has a complaint against another, forgiving each other;

as the Lord has forgiven you, so you also must forgive. And above all these put on love, which binds everything together in perfect harmony. And let the peace of Christ rule in your hearts, to which indeed you were called in one body. And be thankful. Let the word of Christ dwell in you richly, teaching and admonishing one another in all wisdom, singing psalms and hymns and spiritual songs, with thankfulness in your hearts to God.

—Col. 3:12–16 ESV

And whatever you do, in word or deed, do everything in the name of the Lord Jesus, giving thanks to God the Father through him Wives, submit to your husbands, as is fitting in the Lord. Husbands, love your wives, and do not be harsh with them. Whatever you do, work heartily, as for the Lord and not for men, knowing that from the Lord you will receive the inheritance as your reward. You are serving the Lord Christ. For the wrongdoer will be paid back for the wrong he has done, and there is no partiality.

—Col. 3:17–19, 23–25 ESV

Likewise, wives, be subject to your own husbands, so that even if some do not obey the word, they may be won without a word by the conduct of their wives, when they see your respectful and pure conduct. Do not let your adorning be external —the braiding of hair and the putting on of gold jewelry, or the clothing you wear— but let your adorning be the hidden person of the heart with the imperishable beauty of a gentle and quiet spirit, which in God's sight is very precious. For this is how the holy women who hoped in God used to adorn themselves, by submitting to their own husbands, as Sarah obeyed Abraham, calling him lord. And you are her children, if you do good and do not fear anything that is frightening. Likewise, husbands, live with your wives in an understanding way, showing honor to the woman as the weaker vessel, since they are heirs with you of the grace of life, so that your prayers may not be hindered.

—1 Pet. 3:1–7 ESV

Now who is there to harm you if you are zealous for what is good? But even if you should suffer for righteousness' sake, you will be blessed. Have no fear of them, nor be troubled, but in your hearts honor Christ the Lord as holy, always being prepared to make a defense to anyone who asks you for a reason for the hope that is in you; yet do it with gentleness and respect, having a good conscience, so that, when you are slandered, those who revile your good behavior in Christ may be put to shame. For it is better to suffer for doing good, if that should be God's will, than for doing evil.

—1 Pet. 3:13–17 ESV

Wives, submit to your own husbands, as to the Lord. For the husband is the head of the wife even as Christ is the head of the church, his body, and is himself its Savior. Now as the church submits to Christ, so also wives should submit in everything to their husbands. Husbands, love your wives, as Christ loved the church and gave himself up for her, that he might sanctify her, having cleansed her by the washing of water with the word, so that he might present the church to himself in splendor, without spot or wrinkle or any such thing, that she might be holy and without blemish. In the same way husbands should love their wives as their own bodies. He who loves his wife loves himself. For no one ever hated his own flesh, but nourishes and cherishes it, just as Christ does the church, because we are members of his body. "Therefore a man shall leave his father and mother and hold fast to his wife, and the two shall become one flesh." This mystery is profound, and I am saying that it refers to Christ and the church. However, let each one of you love his wife as himself, and let the wife see that she respects her husband.

—Eph. 5:22–33 ESV

Let marriage be held in honor among all, and let the marriage bed be undefiled, for God will judge the sexually immoral and adulterous. Keep your life free from love of money, and be content with what you have, for he has said, "I will never leave you nor forsake you." So we can confidently say,

"The Lord is my helper;
I will not fear;
what can man do to me?"

Remember your leaders, those who spoke to you the word of God. Consider the outcome of their way of life, and imitate their faith. Jesus Christ is the same yesterday and today and forever.

—Heb. 13:4–8 ESV

I hope these scriptures help. As for me, here is my contribution.

Put no trust in a neighbor;
have no confidence in a friend;
guard the doors of your mouth
from her who lies in your arms;
for the son treats the father with contempt,
the daughter rises up against her mother,
the daughter-in-law against her mother-in-law;
a man's enemies are the men of his own house.
But as for me, I will look to the Lord;
I will wait for the God of my salvation;
my God will hear me.

—Mic. 7:5–7 ESV

That is what is called making a joke using scripture. Here is the real opinion.

If you take all the marriage scripture and put it beside all the divorce scripture, you will see a massive abundance of marriage scripture and a massive deficit of divorce scripture.

Christ does not want us to get divorced, just like I said in the "Man vs. Woman" chapter. We as men are the captain of the ship, and the problem starts with us.

In my marriages, I have been a horrible husband, but also in my marriages at times I've been a very good husband. As a man married to a woman, my job is to serve God and do my best to make sure my family has everything they need to serve God.

I believe that a woman's job is to help the man serve God.

Why did both of my marriages end in divorce? Because either I was not serving God or she was not helping me serve God or a mixture of both.

I believe men fall into selfishness and women fall into a form of dominance. Read the Garden of Eden story. This is not new, and if I look at the story of Adam and Eve and then look at both of my failed marriages, I see that it happened before, and I am standing here as a testament that it is happening today. I am not pulling out the flame thrower on everybody to try to hurt them. I'm pulling out the flame thrower to try to get you to never make my mistakes. I beg of you, young man, to be better than I was. I beg of you, young woman, be better than my ex-wives were. Cling to your first love. Cling to that which the moths cannot eat away. Cling to God.

I do not pretend to write new scripture, but I can give you my opinion based on Scripture.

Men, throw away everything selfish just as Christ never displayed selfishness.

Women, throw away everything that is claiming dominance over your husband.

Look at the punishment in the Garden of Eden, and tie that in with what Paul said about husbands and wives. Let the Bible be something you review daily with each other. Confess your faults to each other, be open with one another, and honestly cling to God.

I believe we are at the end of the church age, and what comes next is Daddy walking up the driveway with his belt out. I beg of you to throw away all foolishness.

I do not know if God means for me to ever have another wife. I wholeheartedly understand if he does not give me that responsibility again. But I beg of you, brothers and sisters across the land, learn from my failure and stand where I fell. Reject what I clung to, and cling to what I was supposed to.

SALTY SALT

It is that time again, my family. It is that salt time.

In *Enough Chaos, Volume 1*, I pulled out the flame thrower and hosed down the entire congregation.

As a self-professed plague-bearer, it hurt me to do that. I hate having to be the one to bring all of this to my family. I hate that I have to fill a role that should be naturally taken care of by our pastors and deacons.

I hate what this world has come to.

We get out of our sheltered little high school lives and go to college, tech school, or life with no clue how to battle the dark forces. We have no clue how to spot the darkness. So we fall, but at least we never watched *Harry Potter and the Chamber of Secrets*.

Men fall into debauchery, and women fall into relationship traps.

How did this happen? It's simple. We took the Bible's rules and implemented our own.

If I speak in the tongues of men and of angels, but have not love, I am a noisy gong or a clanging cymbal. And if I have prophetic powers, and understand all mysteries and all knowledge, and if I have all faith, so as to remove mountains, but have not love, I am nothing. If I give away all I have, and if I deliver up my body to be burned, but have not love, I gain nothing. Love is patient and kind; love does not envy or boast; it is not arrogant or rude. It does not insist on its own way; it is not irritable or resentful; it does not rejoice at wrongdoing, but rejoices with the truth. Love bears all things, believes all things, hopes all things, endures all things. Love never ends. As for prophecies, they will pass away; as for tongues, they will cease; as for knowledge, it will pass away.

—1 Cor. 13:1–8 ESV

We took these Bible mandates, these Bible doctrines, this *very* easy list, and replaced it with the self-help steps to enlightenment.

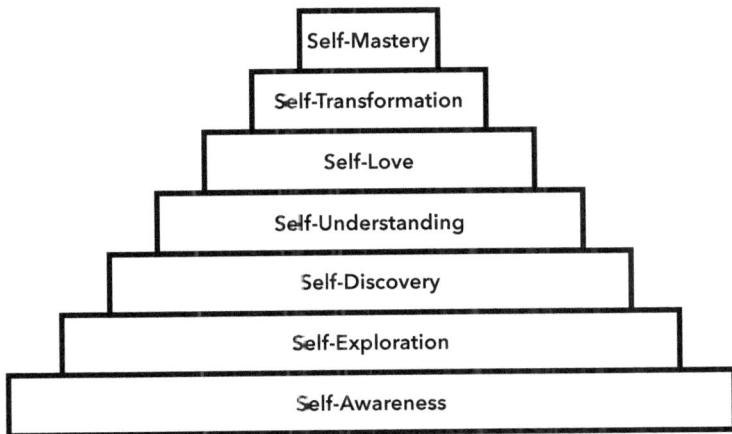

Does everyone see the *glaring* difference between what God said and what some demon whispered to a hippie in the '60s?

The New Age movement teaches self-improvement and

self-reliance to the point that every single female coming out of our culture feels like she is a queen on earth. The problem with that is if she is already a queen, then she already has a kingdom. Where does that leave men?

She cannot come to his kingdom, and she will not abandon her kingdom, so we have a marital stalemate, or worse, we have a marriage that starts broken and stays broken until it just snaps in two. But don't worry, Ms. Queen, at least you still have your kingdom plus alimony now.

When you have no real skin in the game, are you really in the game?

We as the whole church are the bridegroom of Christ, but modern women want that role alone, just like they did in Paul's day, which is why his words tend to sting most females.

Modern men, stop refusing to stand up. Put the lotion back in the bottle. Stop playing games, and cling to the mission God wants you on. We have no desire to return to our first love, God, so we walk down a dark, lonely path. All the while our spouse is behind us fussing because we won't stop and ask for directions (from the Bible), and nope, we just keep on going down the wrong road, taking our families to hell with us.

Female pastors are on the rise, and it's no wonder. All women are queens, and men have been thoroughly subdued.

We dunk our young children and new Christians in a pool or river, and everybody claps, embracing the water baptism, having sold the fire baptism that Christ brought down that very same river. Then we all sit around and preach hippie Jesus who just wants everybody to be happy and specifically wants you to have your best life now. Prosperity gospel is popular and sure does make the coffers nice and fat.

I came to cast fire on the earth, and would that it were already kindled! I have a baptism to be baptized with, and how great is my distress until it is accomplished! Do you think that I have come to give peace on earth? No, I tell you, but rather division. For from now on in one house there will be five divided, three against two and two against three. They will be divided, father against son and son against father, mother against daughter and daughter against mother, mother-in-law against her daughter-in-law and daughter-in-law against mother-in-law.

—Luke 12:49–53 ESV

Personality tests have replaced reading the Bible and sticking to it, and it's no wonder that churches are being led by relational creatures—females. What used to be the does-he-love-me test in *Cosmopolitan* magazine has turned into pastors cashing in on the action, releasing their versions of it, and all the while the Lord has very clearly told us how to act.

We need to throw them (the tests, not the females) out and cling to the Bible. Once we master the lists in the Bible, then maybe it will be okay to play with tests as long as they fit under the Bible.

These tests take the focus off of me trying to be like God wants me to be and makes me accept myself for who I was always supposed to be—sin and all. Silly human, it was never about you being the you that your feeble mind believes you can be. It is about being the Spirit-filled giant that God has planned for you. When you say your opinion matters more than God's, that is 1,000,000 percent narcissistic. That is you at the center of the world, not in the center of God.

Seeing the crowds, he went up on the mountain, and when he sat down, his disciples came to him.

And he opened his mouth and taught them, saying:

Blessed are the poor in spirit, for theirs is the kingdom of heaven.

Blessed are those who mourn, for they shall be comforted.

Blessed are the meek, for they shall inherit the earth.

Blessed are those who hunger and thirst for righteousness, for they shall be satisfied.

Blessed are the merciful, for they shall receive mercy.

Blessed are the pure in heart, for they shall see God.

Blessed are the peacemakers, for they shall be called sons of God.

Blessed are those who are persecuted for righteousness' sake, for theirs is the kingdom of heaven.

Blessed are you when others revile you and persecute you and utter all kinds of evil against you falsely on my account. Rejoice and be glad, for your reward is great in heaven, for so they persecuted the prophets who were before you.

You are the salt of the earth, but if salt has lost its taste, how shall its saltiness be restored? It is no longer good for anything except to be thrown out and trampled under people's feet.

—Matt. 5:1–13 ESV

Women have lost their modesty and compete with each other. Men embrace video games or become sluts, and no wonder. The people who took part in the summer of love are all grown up and have passed their atrocities on to the next generation. Now we are gaining power, and the younger generation has completely lost its mind. Where are the Woodstock hippies? Are they still sitting back and just letting the war happen? Are they not choosing right or wrong but riding in the middle of the road with a joint hanging out of their mouths with marijuana that was grown by the cartels?

Gay marriage in churches is on the rise and no wonder. Look at the sad state of our male role models on TV.

Broken homes are more common than whole ones, and no wonder. Look at the degradation of our churches and the messages coming from the pulpit. Just be the best you can be. No! Not just no, but *noooo!*. We don't get a participation trophy just for showing up. No!

Discipline your body for Christ so you can bear whatever burden gets placed on your shoulders—male and female.

Discipline your mind with the Word of God, the Bible.

Discipline your tongue to say things that are only edifying.

Discipline your ears to hear the truth.

Discipline your heart to love your God.

Do you want eternity? Lay down your life.

Do you want happiness? Embrace those who are sad.

Do you want riches? Bring everything you have to your Father.

Our homes are broken because we reject the Holy Spirit and the gifts that come with him.

But the fruit of the Spirit is love, joy, peace, patience, kindness, goodness, faithfulness, gentleness, self-control; against such things there is no law.

—Gal. 5:22–23 ESV

Our lives are out of control because we have rebelled against the Good Book.

We have no clue what the Lord's feasts are all about, so we cling to a pagan sex fest (Easter) and the day the wise men show up (Christmas), and no wonder all the good spouses live on an island in the Atlantic.

Here is a recap of the feasts from *Enough Chaos, Volume 1*:

#	Feast	Approximate Time	Significance
1	Sabbath	Last day of your week	Lord rested
2	Passover	April	Christ's death
3	Unleavened Bread	April	Sinless (7 days)
4	Firstfruits	April	Christ's resurrection
5	Pentecost, Weeks	June(ish)	Holy Spirit
6	Trumpets	September	Christ's birth
7	Atonement	September	Christ in throne room
8	Tabernacle, Booths	October	Fellowship with Christ

These are not the 12 tribes' festivals; they are ours. The 12 tribes were the servants who brought in the feast so we could dine. They were the librarians protecting the texts so we could check the book out and see the truth. These are my Fathers' feasts. Mine. Maybe they're not yours, but they are *my* Fathers' feasts.

We cling to our family unit, which is not the model set forth by Christ or the apostles. And then when a bump in the road happens, we reject the truth to preserve the family unit. We have sayings such as "blood is thicker than water" and "family first." Both of these are in direct violation of Scripture.

Now great crowds accompanied him, and he turned and said to them, "If anyone comes to me and does not hate his own father and mother and wife and children and brothers and sisters, yes, and even his own life, he cannot be my disciple. Whoever does not bear his own cross and come after me cannot be my disciple. For which of you, desiring to build a tower, does not first sit down and count the cost, whether he has enough to complete it? Otherwise, when he has laid a foundation and is not able to finish, all who see it begin to mock him, saying, 'This man began to build and was not able to finish.' Or what king, going out to encounter another king in war, will not sit down first and deliberate whether he is able with ten thousand to meet him who comes against him with twenty thousand? And if not, while the other is yet a great way off, he sends a delegation and asks for terms of peace. So therefore, any one of you who does not renounce all that he has cannot be my disciple. Salt is good, but if salt has lost its taste, how shall its saltiness be restored? It is of no use either for the soil or for the manure pile. It is thrown away. He who has ears to hear, let him hear.

—Luke 14:25–35 ESV

We have such a false sense of life and the future that we tell our kids, "Grandma is in heaven now, right next to her old cat, Mr. Whiskers," and *nobody* corrects this. It comes from a parent's desire not to hurt the child—by telling them lies.

Grandma is asleep. She's not an angel. She's not with her sidekick cat. She's not playing a harp. She's asleep. She is asleep, awaiting judgment.

Church, we need to change the tires. They're all flat, and eventually your vehicle will totally stop moving.

For those churches that are frothy, for the hungry, for the fire-baptized, for the spouse-loving (at least once a week), for the children-blessing, for the hard-working sons and daughters of my Father, I love you with all my heart and hope you keep on keepin' on. The end is nigh.

I hope and pray this book helps you in some way. I pray we all kneel at the throne together—one church, under God.

www.ingramcontent.com/pod-product-compliance
Lightning Source LLC
Chambersburg PA
CBHW060007100426
42740CB00010B/1428